GATECRASHING

GATECRASHING

GATECRASHING

The Story of 24-7 Prayer in Ibiza

BRIAN HEASLEY

Muddy
Pearl

First published in 2014 by
Muddy Pearl, Edinburgh, Scotland
www.muddypearl.com
books@muddypearl.com

British Library Cataloguing in Publication Data
A catalogue record for this book is available from the British Library

ISBN 978-1-910012-09-3

Design by David McNeill at Revo Creative, Carlisle, Cumbria
Typeset in Minion by Waverley Typesetters, Warham, Norfolk
Printed in Great Britain by Bell & Bain Ltd, Glasgow

In loving memory of James Michael Godward, a great servant to Ibiza and beloved friend and inspiration to us as a family.

To Ellis and Dan who came along for the ride and made it richer, deeper and loads more fun: this story is your story. Gracias mis hijos!

And to Abby and Charlie Clayton, writing the next chapters of God's story for Ibiza – we're so thankful you came.

Tracy this book is your book. It has my name on the front but it was written by both of us. You are my sunshine.

CONTENTS

FOREWORD

FOREWORD

I remember exactly where I was when I read the tabloid headline: 'SODOM & GOMORRAH', it shrieked, name-checking those two infamous biblical cities, synonymous with extreme depravity.

The article went on to describe paralytic drunkenness, drug-fuelled sex, and a date-rape epidemic in and around the pubs, clubs and streets of San Antonio, Ibiza. It was heart-breaking. Thousands of young party-goers seemed to me to epitomise both the lostness and creativity of a generation, looking for fun and finding something else.

I knew that some Christians – maybe most Christians – would share the disapproving tone of the newspaper article, but hadn't Abraham interceded for Sodom and Gomorrah? And Jesus told a parable about God's love for a son who partied too hard. He refused to condemn the woman caught in an act of adultery. He reached out to those in the sex trade; and wept over a generation that was lost 'like sheep without a shepherd'.

'God,' I prayed, clutching the lurid newspaper, 'please – if this is you – open a door for us in Ibiza.'

Life moved on, and a few weeks later I was at a conference talking to a lady at the end of a meeting when she said something that took my breath away: 'I want to invite you to send a team to the island where I live. There are not many Christians. We pray but we feel overwhelmed. The island is called Ibiza.' I blinked and nodded slowly. At that moment the door swung wide and I knew that God was beckoning us in.

And so we sent our first tentative team to San Antonio to 'spy out the land'. They came back with stories of creativity, beauty and opportunity mixed in with the depravity described in the newspaper article. So we sent another team: clubbers, prayer warriors and a couple of Christian DJs. They rented villas, went nocturnal, partied and prayed, enjoying the music and reaching out to those who had collapsed in the street, helping them get home safely, drinking only water from bottles to protect themselves against the pervasive 'date-rape' drug, Rohypnoll.

For several summers we sent 24-7 teams to 'pray, play and obey' on Ibiza. There were miraculous answers to prayer. A television documentary, 'God Bless Ibiza', was viewed by almost a million people. *Rolling Stone* sent a journalist. Teams kept going. The needs kept growing. God kept answering prayers. It became clear that we needed to establish the work long term. We'd never believed in 'hit and run' evangelism. The mission urgently needed year-round presence. But who could head up such an extreme challenge? They would need to be mature, solid Christians who could still relate to young, drunk party-goers. They would have to be flinty pioneers capable of building the mission from almost nothing, and yet they would also need to be people of deep prayer. Worst of all, we had absolutely nothing to offer them. No money. No infrastructure. No home. Just an open door in a place that the tabloids called 'Sodom and Gomorrah'.

Brian and Tracy Heasley rose to that challenge and pioneered 24-7 Ibiza in ways that outstripped everything we could imagine. The story of how God sent them from a village in Norfolk, England to the club capital of Europe remains one of the most dramatic callings I've ever heard. They raised their sons, learned Spanish, led teams onto the streets night after night, reached out quietly, befriending bouncers and club owners and the rich and famous alike until 24-7 Ibiza became trusted as the fourth emergency service on the island. Brian and Tracy also established a drop-in centre with a permanent prayer room, they opened their home continually, and planted a Boiler Room too. The Heasleys are two of the most remarkable leaders I've ever known and their story, recorded here, is a timeless testament to the power of answered prayer.

When I think of the work in Ibiza, I remember the way that the Salvation Army deployed stretcher-bearers to carry the drunks home from London's streets in the 18th century. And I think of C.T. Studd, the England cricketer who gave away his fortune and went as a missionary to China, explaining that, while

> 'Some want to live within the sound of church or chapel bell;
> I want to run a rescue shop within a yard of hell.'

I am so grateful to Brian and Tracy for their sacrifice and for taking the time to write this brilliant new book. As you journey with them through its pages you will be amazed at God's faithfulness and consequently your own faith will grow. You will also learn important principles about contextual, cross-cultural mission, not from academics on the conference circuit but from practitioners who have paid the price night after night, on their knees in the prayer room and in the gutter too. This book will also help you understand the vital relationship between intercessory prayer and incarnational mission and the way that prayer itself can be a paradigm for evangelism.

I hope that you will be inspired to pioneer, to take some even bigger risks, to abandon yourself afresh to the Great Adventure of God for your life. Brian and Tracy's story will also provoke laughter, because the journey of faith is often hilarious, full of the happy-accidents that make life colourful.

I will never forget commissioning Brian and Tracy in a London church at the fifth birthday party of the 24-7 movement. Standing in front of a large crowd I asked why on earth they were giving up a safe life leading a growing church in an English village to go to Ibiza without any security at all. I knew that Brian had many great things he could say in answer to that question. Inspiring things. Intelligent things. Things that might be strategic in drumming up a bit more support. It was a soft pitch of a question, and all Brian needed to do was hit a home run. He opened his mouth to answer, but nothing came out. And then he began to weep. Tracy held his hand tight and he just cried.

Everyone understood the meaning of those tears.

The Heasleys maintained that soft heart through many sub-sequent years of quiet service, mostly away from the spotlight, being yelled at, puked on. And worse. Praying when no one was looking, late at night. Worrying about their boys as all parents do. Enduring the isolation of the long winter months.

And when eventually it was time to come home, Brian and Tracy did it well. There is no lasting success without successful succession, and the Heasleys raised up the next generation who have taken the baton and are growing the mission to a remarkable next level.

Sometimes today, when I ask Brian about Ibiza, he still weeps. No words. Only tears. All these years later. May you sense those tears as you read this book. May you feel them and even share them. May the God of all compassion break your heart, earth your prayers in the dirt, and enlarge your vision beyond the bounds of normal. And may the Lord Jesus who took on flesh two thousand years ago, invade and disrupt our lives again today, gatecrashing our complacency with tears.

PETE GREIG
Guildford, UK
www.EmmausRd.com

PREFACE

PREFACE

Prayer is fascinating, isn't it? The idea that we can communicate with the Creator of the universe, and that he will somehow hear us, is just – outrageous!

But I have seen God answer prayer. I have seen him answer in ways that I expected and in ways that I didn't expect. I have experienced his silence, his immediacy and all that goes in between. Over the last few years I have witnessed God answering prayers in so many ways and I have seen him at work in strange places. Our journey to Ibiza has taught me so much about prayer. It has reinforced my belief that God does hear us – but more than that, it has restored my sometimes wobbly faith to the reality that God not only hears but also intervenes. I have been shown that when we introduce God into any situation stuff happens, things change and lives are transformed.

I believe that if we humble ourselves and pray, God hears from heaven and intervenes. I am not sure that we always get the intervention we expect – but I do believe that every time we pray, something happens.

And in the 24-7 Prayer movement we have found it helps us to do that – to humble ourselves and pray – if we do it together, if we do it intentionally. If we set aside a room for a week where people can come and go, night and day, where they can pray.

That room can be anywhere. We have seen prayer rooms happen in a Missouri brewery, on board a battleship, at a rock in the Zimbabwe desert. We've had prayer rooms in prisons and in some of the oldest cathedrals in the world. We've had prayer rooms in all sorts of churches too – all sorts of sizes, all sorts of denominations. In fact, more than 10,000 24-7 Prayer weeks have been held in a hundred and twenty countries over the last fifteen years, and over 250,000 young people have been through a prayer space in a school here in the UK alone.

We have seen a groundswell of people and communities around the world getting very serious about prayer. There are increasing numbers of people praying wholeheartedly and fervently. This is not a declining situation. People are creating times, spaces and strategies for themselves and other people to connect with God.

They believe that God will listen, that he will intervene – because he does. Stuff happens. They believe that this is the only hope for our world.

People pray, the church prays, I pray.

Last year, I had the privilege of assisting with the Archbishop of Canterbury's 'Journey in Prayer', a pilgrimage which he took before his inauguration. He wanted to mark the beginning of his ministry with a season of prayer. Twelve thousand people turned up over five days at six cathedrals purely to pray. At the end of those five days I thought, 'The church is being forced to its knees.' I wondered if we had begun to realise that all our strategies are useless unless God shows up.

Because whoever is in power, whoever seems to be running the show, it doesn't seem to matter. The only thing that matters is that God shows up. I don't mean we shouldn't take an interest in politics, social engagement or planning for the future. But ultimately the only answer is Jesus. And the only way anything is going to happen is if the church prays.

So I have a passion and a heart for prayer. I want to see God show up and I believe that if we ask he will come. I believe in an interventionist God. We call out and he intervenes.

In my mind I have a picture of what prayer looks like. It is like that *fresco* on the ceiling of the Sistine Chapel, *The Creation of Adam* where God is reaching down to man. Every sinew, every muscle in his arm is stretching out to bring life to Adam. From the red canopy, which signifies heaven, angels and other symbolic characters are looking down on man, backed up behind God, straining to look, almost reaching out themselves, as God seeks to reach in and bring life to man.

It is said that Michelangelo drew his inspiration for this particular *fresco* from the 9th-century Latin hymn *Veni Creator Spiritus*. There is a beautiful line in that hymn, *digitus paterne dextere*, which means 'the finger of the paternal right hand'. That is how I have often pictured prayer – that in the midst of sad and distressing situations, that in the everyday malaise of our everyday existence, the cry of the humble would be heard. And somewhere in all of that muddle and mess, the finger of the paternal right hand would reach down and touch us and the world we live in.

I believe in intervention because I have my own story of intervention. Because it was when I was in prison, when my life was messed up, when my world was crooked and bent out of shape, that God reached down and touched me.

I am the son of a Baptist minister, the second eldest of five boys. When I was young we had a study and an apple tree in the garden and my dad taught us New Testament Greek after tea. But at the age of eleven my mum died from ovarian cancer and I became angry. Very angry. I became involved in drugs, fights and petty theft as I progressed through my teens. This led to me having three or four short spells in prison.

It was my third time in prison, my first night back, and I was on my own in the cell. That didn't happen often. You didn't have to do that – be on your own the first night. But I was on my own. My mind was just in turmoil. I didn't have any drugs, there were heroin addicts banging chairs off doors, I had the pillow over my head and I couldn't sleep. (And to this day I still sleep with a pillow over my head.) I had a Crown Court appearance due and I just couldn't get any sleep.

I remember thinking, 'Now would be a good time to pray, Brian. Now would be a good time to pray.' I didn't have a very articulate language around prayer but I remember saying, 'God, I need peace. God – I need peace ...'

And God broke in. I raised my hand to him and all of heaven stretched down and permeated my cell with peace. A peace that went beyond my questions: my how? When? If? What? Where? Beyond my understanding. It was the peace of God. It was like I called out to God, in my own words, '*Veni Creator Spiritus* – Creator, come.' I called out to God and there he was with all of heaven stretching down to touch me in a cell. I had what I could only call a spiritual experience in a cell. God rocked up.

It was not a conversion experience. I didn't feel the need to give my life to Jesus. There was no follow up, no *Alpha Course*, God just did something spiritual.

Later I found God. I was in a probation hostel in 1990. I'd been taking a lot of drugs again. I had also connected with some Christians:

they had known me as a child and they gave me a Bible. I sat there one day after a particularly heavy drug session and just started to cry, 'God save me. This cycle, this in and out. It feels broken'. And I remember just getting the Bible and reading it. I got to Isaiah 59 and remember reading '*Surely the arm of the Lord is not too short to save*' (Isaiah 59:1).

And at that moment, in that little room in Lightfoot House (known as 'Light-fingered House') the finger of the paternal right hand of God again reached down from heaven, and this time not only touched me, but created new life in me. And I gave my life to God again. I dedicated my life to him.

It was at this point that other Christians stepped in and helped me. A family asked me to come and live with them in Norfolk. They took me out of the subculture that I was in. The church was forgiving and accepting, they enabled me to get through those difficult first three months, six months, twelve months. After that life began to feel normal.

God reached in and lifted me out – his arm was *not* too short to save. He intervened in my life and I am eternally grateful that he did so.

I often draw little doodles of this big hand reaching in and lifting someone out, even now. I am fascinated that God could be bothered to reach down and help us even after all the nonsense we throw his way! I have been captured by a God who reaches in and, in the words of Psalm 40, lifts us up out of the clay and puts our feet upon a rock.

> I waited patiently for the Lord;
>   he turned to me and heard my cry.
> He lifted me out of the slimy pit,
>   out of the mud and mire;
> he set my feet on a rock
>   and gave me a firm place to stand.
> He put a new song in my mouth,
>   a hymn of praise to our God.
> Many will see and fear the Lord
>   and put their trust in him.
>
> Psalm 40

When I read this Psalm, I picture an arm lifting someone out of slime – it's not pretty, but it *is* beautiful.

This picture became even more of a reality to me years later in Ibiza. I was out walking just after midnight, introducing a new member of a mission team to what was about to become her regular work: showing her where the prostitutes hang out, where the drug dealers are, meeting the bar owners and friends, just wandering around trying to put her at ease.

Suddenly, in the water, we spotted a guy who had taken too much Ecstasy.

He kept jumping into the water trying to swim, then gazing at his arms and stroking them, apparently fascinated with the feeling of the water on his skin – a sensation enhanced by the Ecstasy he had taken, but blissfully unaware of the danger he was putting himself in. Twice he jumped into the deep water – twice a Spanish guy dived in after him to drag him out. But then he jumped in a third time. The Spanish guy had gone.

I managed to get to the edge of the pier where he was thrashing about. It was dark and the water was deep. Then all of a sudden we lost sight of him – he went under and all we could see was a trail of bubbles! He was clearly drowning – so I leant over and stuck my arm in the water. I just managed to grab the top of his hair and, with one really big pull and a bit of help from others, managed to drag him out and pin him down until help arrived.

If I hadn't grabbed him he would have drowned. I reached my arm down and pulled him out. I have that lasting image, almost a prophetic picture, of my own right arm, which is tattooed with the name 'Jesus', reaching down to rescue this drowning man.

My prayer is that everyone who is drowning or hurting or lost would reach out and say, '*Veni, Creator, Spiritus*'. Not in Latin, but in their own language, and in their own humble feeble weak way. And that God would break in. That the finger of the paternal right hand of God would stretch down from heaven and touch anyone who calls out to him. I'm so grateful he did it for me.

I believe that those of us who have been touched will start to move beyond just crying out for ourselves, and start to cry out for others. Whether it be in some church hall on a Sunday evening or the streets of Ibiza at four on a Tuesday morning, God's people are calling out, '*Veni, Creator, Spiritus*' – not only for themselves but for the world that needs a touch from the paternal right hand of the Father. That as we pray, we also realise that he will prompt us to use our own arms to reach into slime and drag people out. That as we pray, we will be asked to respond to our own prayers. That our arms will represent the arms of God to others here on earth.

I guess that's what happened to me.

ACKNOWLEDGEMENTS

THANK YOU

Richard and Stephanie Heald – you guys believed in us, put up with my terrible grammar and turned the dream of this book into a reality.

Our families – the Heasleys, the Kerridges, the Dukes and the Moldens – your support, visits, phone calls and care for us meant so much.

Those who gave chunks of their lives to push this work forward – Steve Jeffery, Dawn Beales, Fiona Roberts, Helen Gross, Ben and Becky Edmonds and Bruce Gardiner Crehan. There are no words to adequately express our appreciation for how much you helped to develop the work.

Those who gave up summers – Neil Waters, Tim and Becky Arnold, Jud Sweeney, Emma McQueen, Christine Gardiner Crehan, Claire Ison, Cally G., Kera Package, Anna Saah, Gillian Young, Poppy Williams, Laura Jones, KT Stevenson, Indya Hanlon, Johanna Pahl, Ursina Wiedmer, Bethany Konrad, Michael French, Jillian Davidson, Steph Glenn, Kate Biddle, Kez Clayfield, Timmy Spence, Chris Mahood, Nicki Spence, Heather Hill, Katrina Pyke, Carolyn Skinner, Laura Brown, Stephen McCann, Nick Ashman, Jools Hamilton, Dave Thompson, Tim Hewitt. Thank you for the tireless hours you worked and the fun you added to our community. We couldn't have done it without you.

And everyone who ever came on a summer team or a prayer team – there are too many of you to name individually, but each of you contributed invaluably.

Bob and Clare Short and all at the Anglican church in Ibiza – thank you for your welcome, your prayers and encouragement, and those wonderful church lunches.

Sara Torres – look what your invitation to 24-7 Prayer to come to Ibiza started! A joy to get to know you, pray with you and all those you introduced us to.

Julia Torres – you made so much possible in the early days.

Pete, Sammy, Daniel and Hudson Greig – you guys are an inspiration! You lead the way.

Ian and Jackie Nicholson – Ian, without your visits we would have imploded! Thanks for putting up with my rants!

Billy and Caroline Kennedy – for your care, insight and friendship, and the support of New Community Southampton.

Stevie and Catherine Smyth – for good solid advice and not letting us take ourselves too seriously! And all at Northdown CFC.

Russ and Jan and all at TCF – for your support, contact and encouragement.

Alain Emerson – it was an honour to journey with you, to get to know the wonderful people of Lurgan, and recline at Alan and Gerry's.

Graham and Michele Blake and all at DC3 – thank you for sending us and for welcoming us home.

Adrian and Jenny Eagleson – you pioneered the sending of Irish teams and you helped us so much.

Robb and Sally Harman and your three wonderful sons, Simeon, Ellis and Christie – you helped us catch our breath and cared for us above and beyond.

And finally to Albert, Ange, Abi, Joel and Ben – the holidays, the laughter, the scenes, your friendship means so much to us.

BY SPECIAL INVITATION

BY SPECIAL INVITATION

We left the prayer room at 3 am to walk and talk and see what was happening: within 10 minutes we got offered various drugs on four different occasions – don't know what that says about how we looked!

We then saw a couple having sex on a walkway: loads of people were just walking by and some guys even stopped to watch – it was a very sad and disturbing sight.

We got a call and took a drunk guy back to his hotel in the van, we had a good chat with his two mates.

As we headed back to base, we got stopped by a worker who asked us if we would pray with her, we stopped and prayed with her in the street.

All in all, our little walk only lasted 55 minutes – it's amazing what you can see in that time. We then returned for another intentional encounter with God in the prayer room.

We shared our experience with some of the other team members. I really felt for the girl having sex with that guy in the street – it was so degrading, I'm not judging but just sad. Sad that what should be a beautiful act of intimacy and oneness has been so degraded.

We prayed to get a little more wisdom and understanding as to how to work with this whole area: we struggled to know how to engage with it. Should we have gone up to the couple and asked them to stop? Was it any of our business? Should we have asked people not to stop and stare? Should we have called the police? Lots of questions... This journey often leaves us with more questions than answers, but we laid them all out before God.

After that time of prayer, we ventured back out on to the streets and decided to drop into a club, and pray there. Inside the club on the dance floor there was a group of lads in the middle of the crowd. They had

T-shirts on with comedy names on the back – most I can't repeat here but what really caught my eye was one of the guys had 'Jesus' written on his T-shirt and another had 'Sex God' written on his. They were all dancing in a large crowd of hundreds of people all lost in music and mayhem. Then in the midst of all this madness, on a typical night – where once again we had witnessed a generation 'harassed and helpless like sheep without a shepherd,' lost and searching for fulfillment in all the wrong places, a broken generation trying to fix itself, to the point where all we could do was pray – something extraordinarily prophetic happened. Sex God grabbed Jesus and lifted him up on his shoulders. We stood in amazement at this wonderful picture that, in the midst of all this noise and mess, Jesus was lifted up – he was lifted up above all that was happening, everyone could see him: in that dark moment Jesus became visible.

In that moment I knew Jesus would have gatecrashed that world: not to be a party pooper, not to judge, but just to turn up in an unexpected place and become visible to all.

We had prayed – and then we saw Jesus lifted up!

And that's why we want to continue to pursue prayer and mission: because we want to see Jesus lifted up. We pray and encounter him, we find new levels of significance and security in that place of encounter – and out of that we can do our best to faithfully carry Christ into the world.

This world will be transformed by prayerful people who will carry Christ wherever he asks them to go.

'The vision is *still* JESUS – obsessively, dangerously, undeniably Jesus.'

It felt like gatecrashing someone else's party. When we arrived in Ibiza, we felt awkward and out of place – scantily clad girls and pumping music, streets swaying with superheroes on a stag party and football fans from Bolton – we weren't exactly your obvious fit. We couldn't speak Spanish, we weren't into dance music – I don't even *like* dancing. We must have stuck out like sore thumbs.

But Ibiza is a beautiful island. White sandy beaches, crystal clear sea, blue skies, spectacular sunsets, orange groves, pine covered hills, dark red earth, ancient Spanish villas – it is truly lovely. We discovered hidden treasures, unseen by regular tourists. We loved having tapas in the old medieval town or watching the world go by as we sipped a coffee or a nice glass of wine. It was pure pleasure to walk the dog along the rocks next to the Mediterranean Sea just at the end of the road where we lived. We came to love the Ibiza lifestyle, the relaxed attitude to life and the emphasis that the Spanish placed on family. Most importantly we made friends from all sorts of backgrounds and nationalities on this very cosmopolitan island. We saw why it has long been the haven of the rich and the beautiful. And then also, more recently, of the young and the drunk. And strange as it might seem, it was this second aspect that we felt God was calling us to be involved in.

Every summer hundreds of thousands of holidaymakers arrive – the population of 120,000 is swamped by around 1.5 million visitors over the course of the summer – many of them British, most of them young, and most of them intent on having the best time on their holiday as they possibly can. San Antonio had, until recently, the most pubs, clubs and bars in a square mile in the whole of Europe. Alcohol is expensive in the clubs but in the West End there are offers: BOGOF, all you can drink for a tenner, that kind of thing. There are lots of lively bars and nightclubs – one club not far from San Antonio can hold as many as 10,000 people. It is said that forty thousand Ecstasy tablets are sold in Ibiza every single day of the summer. It's a lucrative trade controlled by rival gangs from UK cities like Liverpool and Newcastle, and from other parts of Europe and North Africa.

Sadly this combination often leads to excess – and the inevitable upsetting scenes of violence and injury and incapacity. In 1998 the UK Vice Consul to Ibiza resigned, very publicly, and was reported to say 'These degenerates are dragging us through the mud.' Ibiza was branded a modern day 'Sodom and Gomorrah' by the British press. 24-7 Prayer took that as an invitation, a challenge if you like, to go to the party island and pray. And there an invitation came: Sara Torres, who was born on the island and had grown up there, met Pete Greig and invited us.

We didn't need a reminder.

But still, we felt like gatecrashers, 'friends of a friend' at a wild party. If we hadn't had an incredibly clear sense of God calling us, inviting us, we would never have considered going.

RANDOM SIGNS, PRAYER AND OBEDIENCE

God speaks to each of us differently. If he is talking to you about mission, about going abroad or doing something in your local area – whether it is a stirring in your heart or a picture or a Scripture or the advice of friends – listen carefully, and talk to people you trust.

For us it was a combination of pointers. It started with a random comment about living abroad, which made an impression on both our minds and just didn't go away. We then began to pray intentionally into our future, and there followed a series of signs and confirmations, some of which were truly bizarre! God managed to speak to us through a friend turning up on our doorstep and presenting us with two kites, the Vengaboys track *We're going to Ibiza*, a homeless transsexual guy, a fifty-something lady in a bikini chasing a beachball, and a National Express advertising campaign!

These random signs happened over a few months, throughout which we were praying together daily, asking God to make clear his plans for us. The signs were accompanied by Bible verses and stories that jumped out at us, the listening advice and prayers of those who were already working and ministering in Ibiza, and the wise words and confirmation of trusted friends and those we were accountable to. And throughout it all, there was a growing sense of God showing us something new that he wanted us to pursue. It took a number of months and there were lots of questions and uncertainties. How would our children cope with such a big move? Were we being responsible parents? What would our friends and families think? Who would take on my role as church leader? How would we survive financially? What exactly would we do when we got there? Would anyone else come and help us? Faith is often scary: 'faith is confidence in what we hope for and assurance about what we do not see' (Hebrews 11:1).

In the end we had to make a move – we had to 'walk by faith and not by sight' (2 Corinthians 5:7 ESV), and start to put things in motion. As with many big life changes, there is a certain unreality in the time between decision made but action still pending. We were living with the little thought 'it's not too late to change our minds,' while ticking off the practical things that needed to be dealt with. Soon came a 'now or never' moment when we realised that if we didn't follow this conviction that God had spoken, we might never have the faith or courage to do anything like this, to really truly step out in faith and follow God's call on our lives.

Ibiza was a place we came to love and appreciate, but the simple truth was that our going was mostly about obedience to what we believed to be God's call. We took the step and found, over the years of prayer and mission which followed, that God was very clearly calling us to join the party in Ibiza, to be his guests, his servants, his representatives. This is the story of those years and some of the things we learned on the way.

SORRY TO INTERRUPT YOUR MEETING

SORRY TO INTERRUPT YOUR MEETING

1

A funny thing happened one night in Ibiza. I met God.

It was about 3.45 am. I was sitting in the prayer room with the team for a quick debrief, as we do at the end of every session. A lot of people were at a Tiesto club night, so we were thinking about winding down for the night. We decided to pray and talk to God.

Just then there was a knock at the door. I went to open it. And there, standing before me was … God.

He said, 'I'm really sorry to interrupt your meeting but we've got a guy out here who needs some help.'

So Ben and I followed. 'God' was a slight chap with short hair wearing a vest, beads, jeans and flip-flops, and carrying a mobile phone.

'God' took us to a man who was lying slumped in the doorway of a club on a busy West End street. We rolled him over. He was an older guy and had a cut over his eye. He had drunk far too much and fallen over in a pub, come outside to catch a breath, vomited all over himself and then fallen into a comfortable, alcohol-induced sleep.

He didn't look great and he definitely didn't smell great – he was a groggy, sweaty, puke-covered, bloodstained mess – but other than this, he was generally okay. So we gently sat him up and then sat either side of him in the doorway to support him. We reassured him, put his wallet in a safe place were he wouldn't lose it, wiped him down a little and tried to find out where he was staying.

We had to listen intently because our doorstep was surrounded. There were about fifteen guys singing football songs – I think they were Bolton fans. A beer bottle bounced off my foot. I chucked it in a bin.

This was our worship. The doorway we sat in was our pew. Unfortunately someone had urinated in it, so Ben unknowingly sat in wee as we worshipped.

Eventually the drunk guy remembered his hotel, and we managed to hear what he was saying. We picked him up, slung his puke-covered arms around our shoulders and carried him to the van. 'God' watched for a bit, but then went back to cleaning up the bar he was working in.

We got the guy into the van and drove him back to his hotel. The hotel staff knew him, so they took over and escorted him to his room.

On our way back, we saw 'God' again. We told him the man was okay and he said, 'Thanks guys. I hate seeing people in that state.'

I was glad God had interrupted our meeting to give us this chance to worship him.

Those words stuck in my mind. That phrase kept going round in my head. I just had to go home and write about it on my blog. It was like a light going on, a kind of epiphany. It made me think.

Maybe when we pray, when we ask him to act, maybe God is saying to us, *'I'm really sorry to interrupt your meeting but we've got a guy out here who needs some help.'* Maybe he is saying it to his church. Maybe it is his call to prayer and mission.

24-7 Prayer has always been about prayer. The clue's in the name. But if you've read a book called *Red Moon Rising* or done time in a prayer room or spent time around the 24-7 Prayer community you'll know that 24-7 Prayer is about the kind of prayer that somehow always leads to mission. It's funny how prayer so often seems to do that.

We draw inspiration from the Moravian movement, where after a particular prayer meeting, in 1727 in Herrnhut, Germany, a prayer watch started and lasted unbroken for over a hundred years. During that time, the tiny community sent out missionaries all over the world. People were stirred to move to Greenland and work with Inuit people, others went to work with Mohicans in North America, and others were prepared to sell themselves into slavery in order to take the life-changing message of Jesus that they had discovered to those who might not have heard it.

In fact some of the first missionaries to be sent out in Protestant church history went out from Herrnhut. Prayer-birthed missionaries. Out of the place of prayer, mission has always happened. We see it in the upper room on the day of Pentecost, and when Peter meditates on a rooftop in Joppa. When people give themselves to prayer and meditation, it seems that God propels them out. Many say that St Patrick's missionary zeal was borne through prayer, while he was in captivity, and that this time of discovering Christ would be the motivator for his return to Ireland to establish the church there. Prayer propelled him out too.

Prayer will inevitably lead to God interrupting our meetings and leading us out into a world that is in need of him.

MELTING ICEBERGS

As we sat on that doorstep, our lovely church back in Diss in England – the songs we sang, the sermons I preached, the passionate prayers we prayed, the concerns of the youth group and the toddler group – all seemed a world away. I don't want to invalidate the place that I had left – but this was just very, very different. This was new territory!

Our time in Ibiza was a bit like having a blank page, where we needed to spend relatively little time on maintaining church – on buildings and meetings and admin – but every opportunity to focus on mission. It made me realise how easy it is to be drawn into a world of church maintenance to the detriment of mission. As a church leader, my time would quickly be taken up with the day-to-day running of church, visiting people, organising, strategising, administering, generally managing. All of it seemed essential, but sometimes it happened at the expense of getting out among people outside of our church world.

The western Christian church is undoubtedly active, but it's also a world of its own – a world with its own music, its own buildings, its own training courses, its own conferences, its own language, its own TV stations and websites, its own books too. This can all take a lot of maintenance.

I do wonder if sometimes the maintenance of church growth slows the momentum of mission? I do wonder if the time we allocate to it is out of proportion. And I do wonder if, while we're busy in our church world, God is knocking on our door saying, '*I'm really sorry to interrupt your meeting but we've got a guy out here who needs some help.*'

Michael Riddell[1] likens churches to groups of people huddling together on an iceberg as it slowly melts. It's uncomfortable to think of church in this way. But I do wonder sometimes. Are we perhaps in denial, just a bit?

If we find ourselves using phrases like, 'We need to engage more with the world', could that be a clue? Could it mean we realise we have *dis*engaged? If we talk about the need to be present, does it suggest we are not very? If we talk about the need to be relevant, does it mean we suspect we have become *ir*relevant?

Many people within the church feel a holy dissatisfaction with the separation of the church from the real world. There is a growing realisation that mission is more than something which zealous people do overseas, evangelism more than something we do on a course, worship more than singing songs and it doesn't only happen in a church service either.

How can we show God's love to our community?

As I travel around teaching about prayer I hear these questions being asked by Christians. And increasingly they are being answered. There are seeds of hope sprouting all over the place: churches engaging, praying and engaging, responding to the knock on the door.

There are food banks, street pastors, drop-in centres, youth clubs, after-school clubs, parent and toddler groups, visits to the elderly. Churches offer debt counselling, marriage counselling, provision for the homeless and they give to overseas aid projects too. The church is growing in levels of engagement all the time. I see a problem, but I also see the problem being addressed. The church has historically been very involved and is now, once again, becoming more involved.

But we mustn't simply go to the other extreme – we must not go from a place of passive prayerfulness to a place of active

---

[1] *Threshold of the Future: Reforming the Church in the Post-Christian West*, Michael Riddell (SPCK 1998).

prayerlessness, replacing one extreme with the other. We need both, at the same time: a life of intimacy and of involvement.

Church was never meant to be a withdrawn community. It was always meant to be a fully integrated part of the world – a group of people who championed creativity, prayer, mission, justice, learning and hospitality.

The German theologian Dietrich Bonhoeffer, just before the start of the Second World War, wrote,

> The restoration of the church will surely come only from a new type of monasticism which has nothing in common with the old but a complete lack of compromise in a life lived in accordance with the Sermon on the Mount in the discipleship of Christ. I think it is time to gather people together to do this ...[2]

We've been talking about new types of monasticism in the 24-7 Prayer community for a while. I recently heard my friend Pete Greig use the phrase 'neo-aposto-monastic communities'. He was playing with words and exploring an idea, but it struck me as an interesting phrase. Actually, the word *aposto* doesn't mean anything, other than 'everything is in order' in Portuguese. But the word *apostolo* means 'sent'.

I like that joining of the two ideas. And with good reason – if you look at the history of true monastic traditions you will find they were communities of people modelling radical discipleship built around a rhythm of prayer and mission that entailed both sacrifice and engagement.[3]

I think this reflects a true picture of what the Church should be: a community that is intimate with God, a community sent by God, a celebrating community, an integrated community, functioning and taking its place in the wider community. An intimate and involved community – a group of people who believe in prayer, who believe in mission, and who do both. People who live with the willingness for their meetings – and actually for their lives – to be interrupted by

---

[2] Dietrich Bonhoeffer, in a letter to his brother (*c* 1935).
[3] You can read more about this in the fantastic book, *Punk Monk*, by Andy Freeman and Pete Greig (Kingsway 2007).

God leading us out into the world: not once but time and time again. To live with this rhythm of withdrawal and response.

DIVINE INTERRUPTIONS

I sometimes think about the disciples of Jesus and how their lives had been interrupted. I picture them in that upper room all those years ago, praying, struggling on in prayer, trying to come to terms with the loss of the one they had loved and served. They knew Jesus. They knew he was risen. They had even seen him ascend to heaven to be with his Father.

The only thing they really understood at that point was that he had told them to wait ... but for what? They'd learned a lot, they lived with him, they'd followed him for a number of years. And now they had been given the task of proclaiming his kingdom to the ends of the earth! They had his teaching to hold on to, they had the ancient scriptures to refer to, they had the sweet memory of the life he had lived out in front of them. But the reality was that there was nothing to tell them about this next step. It hadn't been done before. They had no map and no manual – just a promise.

A promise of 'the Spirit'. A promise that if they waited he would come. But who was he? One who comes alongside, a person? It makes more sense now, in the light of history, but at that precise moment they were probably very confused, wondering, 'What is this all about? What does it mean?' All they could do was wait and pray and hold on to the hope which fuelled that prayer. Jesus had spoken, he had told them to wait and so that's all they could do.

And then it happened. *Their* meeting was interrupted. The sound of a rushing wind filled the room. I always imagine someone looking round and thinking '*Who left the doors open?*' or '*Didn't know it was going to be stormy today*'. Even in Jerusalem, the holy city, fire did not descend onto the heads of people in a prayer room very often. But there it was, in that room, blazing, burning. They must have realised pretty quickly that this was God. This was a theophany – an appearance of Old Testament proportions. The God who could only be described as fire and wind was now in the room! The Holy Spirit came and revealed himself in what sounded like wind and looked like fire!

This was an amazing interruption.

They had no plan, no guide book, just a promise and the instruction to wait. And then he turned up. God was faithful: he sent his Spirit, the meeting was interrupted and the disciples were empowered.

What happened next is something that has always filled me with faith and excitement and an overwhelming sense of awe. The interruption led to a response. The God of heaven and earth pours his Spirit out on what was, in effect, 'the Early Church' and they respond by stumbling out into the market place.

This first outpouring of the Spirit did not result in a Holy Spirit hotspot being created, a gathering point for people to travel to and bathe in the glory. This was an incarnational God sending his Spirit so that his church could live incarnate in his world. The first outpouring of God's Spirit resulted in the propelling of its first recipients out into the market place. No mould, no model: just a stumbling band of disciples who had waited, allowed their lives to be interrupted, responded to the interruption and gone on an incredible journey – a journey of prayer and mission.

In those few moments Peter gets inspired, strange languages are spoken, people are mistaken for drunks, the gospel is preached and the lost are saved. The church's first day was a good one. It began that day with simple preaching but soon led to widows being fed, orphans being looked after, fields being sold, possessions being shared, men travelling to other nations, and a general sense of transformed and active lives of faith.

GOD'S LITTLE 'AHEM'

It's here I think we start to see an emergent pattern, a way of being. It actually looks like at that moment their lives became lives of interrupted-ness. The church's first foray into the world was one of responding to the Spirit's interruptions. They didn't initiate: they prayed, and God showed up. Could we learn something from that?

This kind of interrupted life does make me remember my childhood – as I said, I'm the son of a pastor and one of five boys. I remember being taken to people's homes for Sunday lunch, and on the doorstep my father saying, 'All right boys, no messing around'. If at some point we started to get a little boisterous or rude, he would cough – just a little *ahem-ahem* – and we would know. There were no words, just a quiet cough. But we knew these gentle coughs: they stopped me in my tracks and demanded a response from me.

We have two sons and I do the same. They respond to my little *ahem*. They know that there's something about what they are doing, or are about to do, that I want to interrupt.

I like to think of it like that – that as the early church grew, they listened to the little *ahem* of the Spirit, they began to move to a rhythm of interrupted-ness.

A few days after the first interruption Peter and John went up to Gate Beautiful in Jerusalem, as they had done many times before, and this time they heard their father's *ahem*. They responded. They didn't initiate, they responded. They heard the prompt and they went with it. There was no handy instruction sheet in fifteen languages on how to pray for healing for a lame man at the gate of a temple. It could have all ended in failure. They could have looked very stupid. But they stepped up and stepped out. And in that moment of responsiveness, God showed up, the man was healed and the kingdom was advanced.

Throughout the Bible we are witnesses to people's lives being interrupted by God and to their subsequent responsiveness to God. Moses was interrupted at the burning bush. David's life as a young shepherd was interrupted when Samuel came to anoint him. Mary's betrothal to Joseph was interrupted by an angel. Matthew's life as a tax-collector and Peter's fishing business were interrupted by Jesus. But each of them responded and followed God's call, his *ahem*.

I love the stories of Jackie Pullinger, Bill Hybels, and Rick Warren – humble individuals who had the gumption to respond to the little *ahem* of God. God interrupted their lives too, gave them strategies, led them into new things and guided them in the forward momentum of his church here on earth.

But I'm sometimes worried by how quickly these stories get turned into formulæ. They were written in hindsight as a record of responsiveness and obedience to God's interruptions. And God does things differently every time. Joshua didn't cross the Jordan the same way that Moses crossed the Red Sea. The children of Israel didn't take all the towns and cities in the Promised Land the same way that they took Jericho. Paul didn't use the same methods to plant churches in all the different cities he went to. They didn't land on an effective model, they just listened to the prompts and coughs and *ahem*s of the Spirit. They responded.

NOT A FORMULA

This is a book about prayer and mission – but it's not a formula. Sure, I try to give some tips and insights which I hope will help you. But if you take one thing away from reading this book, take with you the call of God for you to live a life of responsiveness to his interruptions. Not a formula, but a call to a life of prayer and mission.

Of course we can gain wisdom and learn from the principles and ideas of other people's journeys, but they must never replace our dependence on the Holy Spirit. God is looking for people who will be *inspired* by the stories, and who will depend on him to lead them in the unfolding of their *own* story, of *his* story in *their* lives. God is not looking for us to create Christian formulæ, but to walk, perhaps stumbling a little, in response to him on our own interrupted journeys.

Why do we turn other people's stories into a formula or rule? Why do we look more at what, why and how they did it, than at what influenced and guided them on their journey?

Perhaps it's fear and insecurity that causes pastors to look for a model, a pattern, a rule, rather than finding out what works for them in their own situation. Perhaps we are looking for a shortcut. Perhaps we are simply overwhelmed by the task. Or maybe, at a personal level, we are all just genuinely hungry to see a move of God and we will try anything to see it happen. I would say that hunger for revival is probably the primary motivating factor when it comes to our pursuit of models. Perhaps there is a genuine hunger and longing to see God move in our lives but we don't know how – or where – to start.

But God looks for dependence on him, not on a model. And that always seems to start when we come to the end of our rope or realise that all our knowledge, reading and experience will count for very little if we don't have a dynamic, active and responsive prayer life that makes us attentive to God and his leading. God shows up when we, like the psalmist, start longing for God as the deer pants for the water.

A man called Charles Spurgeon once said: 'All that a college course can do for a student is coarse and external compared with the spiritual and delicate refinement obtained by communion with God … all our libraries and studies are mere emptiness compared with our closets. We grow, we wax mighty, we prevail in private prayer.'[4]

I love that phrase '*delicate refinement*'. As we spend time in his presence I believe we are *delicately refined* to the needs of the world, yet this *delicate refinement* takes time.

> Don't look for shortcuts to God. The market is flooded with surefire, easygoing formulas for a successful life that can be practiced in your spare time. Don't fall for that stuff, even though crowds of people do. The way to life – to God! – is vigorous and requires total attention.
>
> Matthew 7:13–14   (*The Message*)

What you have here is a book about a pair of interrupted lives and how we went on a missional journey borne in prayer. It hasn't been easy, it is vigorous and requires our total attention. But it was as if God knocked at the door of our lives and said, '*I'm really sorry to interrupt your meeting but there's a guy out here who needs some help.*' For us that guy was Ibiza! And we had to respond.

This is our interrupted journey. As we look back, some of it makes sense. Other bits don't. We didn't get wind and fire, we haven't seen the same as the early disciples. But we became a family on a journey and learned loads. These are lessons we learned on our journey. We wanted to share them with you because we are grateful to God that he still wants to interrupt lives and take people on journeys.

Helen Keller once said, '*Life is either a daring adventure or nothing.*'

---

[4] *Lectures to my Students*, C H Spurgeon (Zondervan, 1954).

God wants to interrupt all our lives and see his church live a life of responsiveness to him. For that, he is a looking for a prayerful, missional people.

We believe God may want to interrupt your life. Our prayer is that as you read our story, you will hear his little *ahem*, his unique call for you. It will be different to ours. But it will be every bit as exciting.

GAY MAN DANCING

GAY MAN DANCING 2

I could tell it was going to be a weird morning from the moment I ventured into the toilets of the club. A guy in a wig and ballgown stood at the urinal next to me, hitched up his skirt and had a pee!

It is a hot, humid June day in Ibiza. The music is pumping, the bodies are moving, the lights are flashing and the sound system is blaring. I am standing in the middle of Space, one of Ibiza's top clubs. A few thousand guys in tight T-shirts and a variety of outfits surround me, lost in the music and each other, moving on the dance floor or lounging by the various bars.

I somehow manage to fight my way through the crowd to the bar and order a diet Coke for Tracy and I. But my request is lost in translation and I find myself clutching two large Jack Daniels and Cokes instead. It was such a stress to get served in the first place, I can't be bothered to fight my way back to change my order. We pray that the whiskey will somehow miraculously turn into water. It doesn't, but we drink it anyway. I make a mental note that, to stop this kind of mistake happening, I must improve my Spanish – morning drinking isn't helpful here.

Thirty minutes earlier we had dropped our children off at the beginning of the school day, just like normal parents on a normal Tuesday. We had been packing lunches, making breakfast and harassing the children to hurry up, driving on the edge of the speed limit to ensure they were not late. Now, at 9.30 in the morning, I have already spurned approaches from two middle-aged guys in fitted designer shirts while watching another forty-something guy dancing around in nothing but tight black hot pants and a gorgeous diamante collar. I came to be a missionary but here I am watching a gay man dancing.

This is weird.

I'm *way* out of my comfort zone. This is completely beyond anything I have ever experienced in the past. This is new land, new terrain. I'm fascinated, intrigued and deeply uncomfortable. We weave through the extensive cavernous club down into the basement where we see dancers on stage, one performing oral sex on another. It feels very dark and makes me very uneasy and I want nothing more than to leave the whole place immediately. But for now we move back upstairs to another area of the club where it is physically, but also spiritually, lighter.

I can't dance and I don't go to clubs much. I'm not gay but I'm not homophobic either. Yet I am starting to feel a high degree of discomfort with my surroundings – almost more than in any of my prison experiences, or at any time since.

I move closer and closer to Tracy, I am putting my arm around her, holding her hand and generally making it very obvious that I am straight, but that doesn't entirely prevent another advance. Why me? Do I look gay? Strangely I find myself wondering why it is only the older, less attractive guys: am I not handsome enough for the young buff ones? Before I know it I am having body image issues, thinking I should go to the gym more, maybe even buy some anaconda skin shoes.

This had all started the previous evening when a Christian friend who is a DJ invited us to the club he was playing at. Yet again my poor Spanish let me down. I was sure that he said it would be a '*guay*' day. *Guay* in Spanish means cool, but now I realise that he was actually trying to give me a heads-up by explaining to me in English that it was a gay day at Space. He'd wanted us there because he doesn't get a lot of support and we really believe in supporting artists, standing with them, praying and encouraging them to work out their giftings wherever God leads them.

We had been living in Ibiza for four months at this point. So there I was, standing in a club, feeling a very long way from the sleepy medieval Norfolk market town of Diss!

I have been to Space lots of times since then and enjoyed it – it is an artistic, spacious, airy club. Something about being there makes you feel good. But my first time there was a weird day for me.

RETHINKING PILGRIMAGE

And there, in the middle of Space, in the midst of all my inner struggles, something struck me: *this* is where prayer and mission takes you.

It's a form of pilgrimage. A pilgrimage of change. Of giving up everything that is familiar and known and comfortable and ending up in the unknown, in unexpected places along the way. Places and encounters which confront me with who I am, what I believe and what I think about others.

It isn't so much about the great things we are going to do. It is about what God is going to do in us, the lessons he will teach us, the people we will meet and the situations we will find ourselves in. It is about all this combining to change us, to bring about a transformation in our attitudes to challenge us with difficult questions, to give us life and life to the full. That's what this is about.

We had become pilgrims on a journey of prayer and mission and somehow this had brought us to Space in Ibiza in the middle of a Tuesday morning.

When I was young a copy of a painting hung on our living room wall. It was of the Pilgrim Fathers boarding the *Mayflower* at Southampton to begin their journey to a new land. When I think of pilgrimage, that's the image that jumps to mind – an image of people who are travelling toward a specific destination, tired, weary travellers getting on a boat for some distant destination, braving the elements – enduring hardship but enduring in order to reach the promised land.

I had never really thought of myself as a pilgrim. But today it was clear, almost an epiphany! And increasingly, as our time in Ibiza unfolded, I was struck by the verse 'Blessed are those whose strength is in you, whose hearts are set on pilgrimage' (Psalm 84:5). It was at that moment, in that club, that I realised my heart was set on pilgrimage – a pilgrimage of prayer that was intrinsically linked to mission, that would push us out into mission.

The usual understanding of pilgrimage is a journey made by Christians – and other religious people – towards a specific location, a shrine, a monument, a temple or a church. Yet there are other kinds of pilgrim for whom a specific location is not always necessary. That's me – it's less about a destination and more about the journey itself. In early Celtic Christianity one group of pilgrims were Irish evangelist monks called the *Peregrinari Pro Christo* (Pilgrims for Christ), also known as 'white martyrs'. These guys were pilgrims who left with the intent simply to wander. This sort of pilgrimage was an ascetic religious practice: leaving the monastery, the clan and home for an unknown, yet-to-be-specified destination – and they did this in complete trust of divine providence.

There are a number of reasons I like the sound of these guys. At the most superficial level they were Irish, and so am I. But I also like the fact that their journeys, which began as aimless wanderings, often resulted in the establishing and development of new abbeys and in spreading Christianity throughout the pagan population of Britain and continental Europe. They prayed and went wherever the wind blew them, and their prayers tended to lead them into darkness. I realised that what we were doing – praying then being led on a mission – really was nothing new!

Those early monks gave themselves over to the leading of God and he led them to new places and provided them with new adventures. We had done the same. We had arrived at that point where we could say, 'Not my will, but your will be done'. We had asked God to lead us, to take us to new places. We had set our hearts on pilgrimage and he had led us to a club called Space.

UNSETTLED

There's a story in the Bible that for me carries a note of sadness: Terah, Abraham's father, sets out for the Promised Land. He goes on a pilgrimage, and that is what is in his heart.

> Terah took his son Abram, his grandson Lot son of Haran, and his daughter-in-law Sarai, the wife of his son Abram,

and together they set out from Ur of the Chaldeans to go to Canaan. But when they came to Haran, they settled there.

Genesis 11:31

Canaan was the Promised Land, and eventually Abram would go there and possess it. In the very next chapter we hear about Abram and his family going to Canaan: '... they set out for the land of Canaan, and they arrived there' (Genesis 12:5).

Abram and his family arrived, but Terah never did! It was in Terah's heart to go to Canaan, it was originally Terah's dream, Terah's pilgrimage, but he arrived at Haran and settled there! Haran wasn't the Promised Land. It wasn't the original destination of his pilgrimage, yet somehow he had stopped and if you read a little further it says: 'Terah lived 205 years, and he died in Haran' (v 32).

How many of us have set our hearts on pilgrimage and settled half way? We have started out for the Promised Land, our hearts full of vision, excitement and anticipation, yet somehow on the journey we have settled and are on the verge of dying in our own personal Haran. Maybe we are guilty of living on 'One Day Isle': 'One day I'll do this', 'One day I'll go here', 'One day I'll give this'. Before you know it the 'one days' have all added up, they have become a decade or even longer, and we become aware that life has crept up on us and we have settled and we're going nowhere. We no longer have pilgrimage in our hearts. We have stopped growing, stopped moving – and started dying.

These verses had really challenged us before we set out on our journey to Ibiza. We were doing all the right things, working hard, serving the Lord and enjoying living in a good place. Yet somehow we were in danger of settling and dying.

That's not what God is looking for. He really doesn't want us to play it safe, he wants us to set our hearts continually on pilgrimage, on following him wholeheartedly, all the way. He doesn't want us to end up settling in Haran and dying there. Maybe as we set our hearts on pilgrimage he will cause us to face our prejudices, to look deeper into ourselves and realise that in many ways it's our attitudes and hearts that are killing us rather than our geographical location.

STRETCHED

On this pilgrimage, this journey in prayer, I have started to realise it's more about him and less about me. It's Christ being formed in me, as it says in the letter to the Ephesians, '... we are his workmanship, created in Christ Jesus for good works, which God prepared before-hand, that we should walk in them' (Ephesians 2:10 ESV). It's me becoming who I was meant to be, learning and growing through life more than through some form of classroom teaching or advanced discipleship course. It's about living with my heart set on pilgrimage, being a pilgrim and striving to remain a pilgrim, journeying and allowing the journey to change me, allowing the journey itself to train me.

Right there, in that club, on that morning, is where the real became more real. Where my mind got opened. I realised that if I was going to grow and enjoy this journey of prayer and mission then I had better let the God who guides me challenge and provoke me in order that I could be more like his Son Jesus.

This is the heart of our journey.

We learn better when we are stretched. We don't like it but we really learn better when times are hard. So here I was on a very steep learning curve. 'Stretched' really doesn't begin to describe it. We had set out and determined to follow wherever he led and this place was where the baby steps of our pilgrimage had taken us.

My own prejudices were jumping out at me. Surely this wasn't the place for a Christian to be! I mean when I think of missionary journeys, this is not what springs to mind. What could God possibly want me here for? Why hadn't he sent me to Africa or India to work in an orphanage or do something a bit more worthwhile? I can't remember many missionaries who started out in a gay event in a club with a Jack Daniels and Coke in hand. What was it all about? We had prayed, given ourselves to mission, and ended up here!

LESSON OF LOVE

As I delved deeper into myself and tried to find some room to think amongst all the energy and noise, I realised this episode in the journey had become a lesson. The lesson I was learning and am continuing to learn was simple. The lesson was love. I had somehow been propelled on a journey of love.

It was like that wonderful moment in the film *Bruce Almighty* where Bruce (Jim Carey) is sitting with God (Morgan Freeman) in a diner. They are having a conversation and Bruce is trying to get his head around his new powers when God says, 'Come walk with me'. God had responded to our desire to be involved in prayer and mission by saying, 'Come walk with me' and that walk was going to take us on a journey of love.

In that instant, I had to remind myself that God passionately loved everyone in Space just as much as he loved me. Absolutely no difference. This was the moment I became aware that I was on a pilgrimage of love, of learning more about the love of God: his love for me, his love for others and his passion for life and humanity.

Our prayer lives should cause our love for others to grow. In his book the *The Wounded Healer*, Henri Nouwen says this:

> The Christian leader must be in the future what he has always had to be in the past: a man who has to pray and has to pray always, a man of prayer ...
>
> For a man of prayer is in the final analysis the man who is able to recognise in others the face of the Messiah and make visible what was hidden, make touchable what was unreachable.[1]

As we start to see the Messiah in the face of others our love for them must inevitably grow.

I am constantly struck by God's passion for people. How that passion is not diminished by circumstance and is incredibly strong regardless of who you are or what you are doing. This love I felt that morning transcended behaviour or appearance. It was strong and almost overwhelming. My heart was moved, probably expanded somewhat. I couldn't really put my finger on it at first but just started to notice a shift inside me, a warmth, a contentment, a real sense of this being where we were meant to be. This new territory needed

---

[1] *The Wounded Healer: In our own woundedness, we can become a source of life for others*, Henri J M Nouwen (Darton Longman & Todd 1979, 2014).

more love, but primarily it needed me to have more love! I had a Holy Spirit moment of growth that was totally unexpected. That moment could be best described as a 'gentle expansion'. Somehow in the mayhem of music, images and sexuality on display, the gentle dove of the Spirit came and touched my heart, and it grew.

I love that piece in Song of Songs: 'Many rivers cannot quench love' (Song 8:6–7), describing how God's love is so strong and beats with an intensity we will never be able to match. It is so intense that he would give his son for this picture of broken humanity that I was confronted with. This overwhelming unstoppable force of God's love was being planted into my own heart. I was starting to feel a miniscule part of that love. In prayer my ordinary heart was being softened with love.

I am ordinary. The places and situations I have found myself in aren't always ordinary. But I am as ordinary as the next man. I struggle with all sorts of things – at times I'm jealous, I'm lustful, I'm grumpy, I'm aggressive, I want to give up, I'm prone to laziness, I can be judgmental and harsh. I like watching mindless television programmes, I enjoy walking the dog, smoking the occasional cigar and drinking beer. I can ignore my wife for a football game and become a zombie to the world when I am on my laptop. I'm ordinary.

Of course one man's 'ordinary' can be another man's 'weird', so you always have to be careful how you brandish this word about. But genuinely I feel ordinary. I've just set my heart on a prayerful relationship with God and become aware that, despite my flaws and ordinariness, God has and does touch me with his love in order that I can express it to others.

I left the club with a real and growing understanding of God's passion for others and with an awareness that, in my ordinariness, I could be a carrier of his love to others. That we as a couple had a message and that message was love. Sounds too simple doesn't it? Even slightly hippyish and wishy-washy. Maybe I should buy the sandals, grow my hair, wear lilac and hug people a lot. Or maybe not.

This isn't a shallow unearthly love. I hope that you will grow to understand that prayer and mission means to carry a message of love that can be very real, very earthy and extremely messy. Love conquers all, but it doesn't just conquer all with a flower in its hair. It conquers all by getting dirty, it conquers all with sacrifice, it conquers all with humility and it conquers all by the carrier of the love being aware that I am just a vessel beholden to a deeper love, a love that I must serve, a love that I must allow to lead and a love that I will gladly allow to master me. That is the love and passion of God.

Leon Morris explains it like this:

> The Christians thought of love as that quality we see displayed on the cross. It is a love for the utterly unworthy, a love that proceeds from a God who is love. It is a love lavished upon others without a thought of whether they are worthy to receive it or not. It proceeds rather from the nature of the lover, than from any merit in the beloved. The Christian who has experienced God's love to him while he was yet a sinner has been transformed by the experience. Now he sees men in a measure as God sees them. He sees them as objects of God's love, as those for whom Christ died. Accordingly his attitude towards them is one of love, of self-giving agape. He comes to practice the love which seeks nothing for itself, but only the good of the loved one.[2]

PRAYER ALTERS OUR VISION

With the sights I see I have to realise his passion, I have to see people on my journey through God's eyes, I have to comprehend that he feels for my world and for your world. On my journey I must realise he has the same passion for the man we took home last night who we found propped up against a car park wall, snoring, covered in vomit and stinking of beer as he has for me. I may look on and think to myself, 'I would never get into that state', somehow invoking a false sense of pride and worthiness that I deserve God's love more than this guy. I need to realise just how much of a lie that is, and how that in my Father's eyes we are both equally loved.

---

[2] *1 Corinthians: An introduction and commentary,* Leon Morris (IVP 2008), p 181.

He feels the same passion for the three girls we took home the other night – in a complete muddle from ketamine, vulnerable and a little bit scared – as he does for my wife Tracy. Even though Tracy is the apple of my eye and the one I have chosen to give my love to in as intimate a manner as is possible, I must not somehow think she deserves his love more because she is the centre of my world.

He feels the same passion for the alcohol-fuelled groups of men and women walking through the West End of San Antonio wearing as little clothing as possible as he does for my two sons, Ellis and Dan. Wow! That's a hard one: how could God love these people more than my innocent children?

He feels the same passion for the young teenage couple having sex in full view right on the main walkway along by the seafront at five in the morning as he does for the people I used to go to church with. Can that be right?

He feels the same passion for the guy who can hardly stay on the pavement at nine in the morning who, when I ask if he knows where he's going, just says, 'Anywhere I can get another drink'. He feels the same passion for this man as he does for people calling out for more of his Holy Spirit. But surely those who seek what is pure are loved more than those who seek to pollute their bodies?

He feels the same passion for the girl throwing up in the street, who has somehow lost her knickers, as he does for the cleaner who will clear it up while she's sleeping. The injustice of it! The one making the mess is as loved as the one cleaning up the mess.

He feels the same passion for the guy with the wild staring eyes, grinning away and chewing his lip, who is still dancing thanks to the Ecstasy he's taken to keep him awake and help him enjoy his night out.

He feels the same passion for the drug dealer who sold him the Ecstasy.

In all humility I must remember that he feels the same passion for me, in my own broken, sinful state, as obvious or as hidden as that might be to anybody else.

In any exploration of prayer in a missional context, you will soon realise that it has to happen in a context of love. Prayer will lead us to discover the passion God has for others and compel us to do something about it. Initially it's not about where you are and what you do. It's about setting your heart on a pilgrimage of prayer and mission, allowing God to open your eyes, and being willing to go wherever he takes you on his journey of love. It's not an easy journey. It's one that continually throws up questions, hard questions, questions that provoke us to think about our own judgmentalism and our own levels of grace.

My journey began there in Space. I learnt that day not to be so judgmental. Jesus had words of contempt for people who looked down on other people's lifestyle choices – thinking that they were of greater worth because, in their eyes, they'd got it right. His passion for the gay man dancing was revealed to me.

> Do not judge, or you too will be judged. For in the same way as you judge others, you will be judged, and with the measure you use, it will be measured to you.
>
> Matthew 7:1–2

I can't make judgments on people because they live a different way to me. I need to see people as God does – people he loves passionately, just as he loves me. I need to love them.

We need to ask God for his love for others. This prayer has to be prayed repeatedly and often: 'God help me to see people as you see them'. Discovering God's love, his passion for messy people, and trying to express some of that passion to them through our lives on our journey, is the key to mission.

Bob Pierce, founder of the international aid agency World Vision, once said, 'Let my heart be broken by the things that break the heart of God'. That's similar to what I am saying about discovering God's passion for others.

It was said that Pierce 'prayed more earnestly and importunely than anyone else I have ever known. It was as though prayer burned within him. ... Bob Pierce functioned from a broken heart' (Richard Halverson http://en.wikipedia.org/wiki/Robert_Pierce). I think that's what happens – our hearts get broken for the world and we start to function out of that broken heart.

I soon began to find myself crying more. Every time I was asked to speak about the work in Ibiza at some point in my talk I would break down. I found this a little unsettling at first but then realised it was God. I was crying because he was crying. When I articulated what I felt about Ibiza and all the brokenness I saw, I would break a little bit more. It wasn't an inconsolable place, it was a place my heart had arrived at in prayer. As I prayed, my love grew and in growing my passion became increasingly linked to God's passion.

On the journey of prayer and mission we will get closer to knowing God's heart for others. Yes – it's a vulnerable place to be. Yes – there will be times when you feel he's taken everything you call your own, stripped you bare, messed with your head, provoked you and got you mixed up in something you feel is too difficult. But it's a blessed place to be. It's the way of love.

Love never gives up.
Love cares more for others than for self.
Love doesn't want what it doesn't have.
Love doesn't strut,
Doesn't have a swelled head,
Doesn't force itself on others,
Isn't always 'me first,'
Doesn't fly off the handle,
Doesn't keep score of the sins of others,
Doesn't revel when others grovel,
Takes pleasure in the flowering of truth,
Puts up with anything,
Trusts God always,
Always looks for the best,
Never looks back,
But keeps going to the end.

1 Corinthians 13:4-7   (The Message)

PRAYER WALKING

PRAYER WALKING 3

One quiet night in July we took a walk out along the harbour wall to pray. We could see the whole of the bay of San Antonio. It was beautiful and peaceful and a great place to pray at four in the morning.

We walked out on this lovely wooden walkway with lights stretching the whole way along out into the darkness. I enjoyed the picture it presented me with, that sense of light piercing darkness, walking in the light yet being surrounded by darkness. The walkway is built on rocks and that spoke to me about being on a firm foundation. Simple analogies. Yet when we engage with prayer in a physical way it can seem so much more alive.

On our quieter evenings, when not much was happening, we would go walking and praying, and have our faith for our neighbourhood restored!

PREPARING THE GROUND

From the very beginning of our time in Ibiza, we prayer walked. The summer teams that had preceded us had all walked and prayed loads, so it seemed natural for us to continue. It was something we kept up for seven years.

Several times each week, we would drop the children off at school and then carry on to San Antonio to pray. We didn't have an office or a centre at that time, no prayer space to go into, nowhere we could just turn on some music and pray in private. So we prayer walked around the town.

Our prayer walks were not dramatic, simply a walk and talk between Tracy, myself and God. We walked with eyes open, taking turns to speak to God in a normal voice, agreeing with each other, sometimes interrupting one another. To anyone watching, we would have looked like a couple just out for a stroll and a chat in the sun.

At first we walked through the town but everything was still new and interesting, and we would get distracted. I remember one day spotting a sale on at Diesel jeans and the next moment we were flicking through the rails inside the shop! To help us, and especially me, to avoid distraction we decided instead to walk around the borders of the town. We pictured ourselves as being a bit like Joshua and the children of Israel walking around Jericho.

Often it was just Tracy and me, praying. In the first few months we didn't know anyone living in the town and we hadn't yet experienced the transformation from quiet town to party zone that would take place in the summer with the arrival of thousands of tourists and seasonal workers. All we knew was what we had gleaned from stories we had heard and that infamous documentary that provoked a British newspaper to hail Ibiza as the new Sodom and Gomorrah.[1]

Aware that we were probably not the obvious choice of people for mission in an area revolving around the 18-to-30s party scene, yet still sure that God had led us here, we turned to prayer, believing that God had a plan for the place and fearfully conscious that this was only going to come about with God's help.

I remember hearing the story of a friend, Kelly Green. Kelly was with 24-7 Prayer in Mexico, and she prayer walked around a border-town brothel enclave called Boystown before she was able to do anything – even to go inside the walls.

> I didn't have any great brilliant strategies on how to reach Boystown. But I knew I could pray. I moved down here, didn't know anyone, didn't know what to do. So I began to prayer walk around the walls of Boystown. Fifteen months, all I did was pray. And I felt like a bit of a failure. My prayers were like 'God, do you hear this, this time? Because I still don't know the names or stories of anyone who lives inside those walls'. Fifteen months, nothing but praying? I felt crazy.
>
> *Kelly Green*

---

[1] *http://www.independent.co.uk/arts-entertainment/its-a-disgrace-1195206.html.*

Often it is after consistent and determined prayer when seemingly nothing happens, that things suddenly begin to change.

For us it wasn't quite the same as it was for Kelly. When we came to Ibiza, we came on the back of other people's prayers. The summer teams had prayer walked for six years before us. And so had the local churches for many years before them. We knew we had to pray, but we were starting from further on, from a position of strength, adding another layer of prayer to what was already there.

KNOWING YOUR LAND

There is something biblical about walking the land. After the death of Moses, the Lord says to Joshua:

> 'Now then, you and all these people, get ready to cross the River Jordan into the land I am about to give to them – to the Israelites. I will give you every place where you set your foot, as I promised Moses. Your territory will extend from the desert to Lebanon, and from the great river, the Euphrates – all the Hittite country – to the Mediterranean Sea in the west.'
>
> Joshua 1:1–4

God was specific about the geographical area he wanted the Israelites to have, he was clear about the actual boundaries. Reading this led us to ask ourselves the question, 'What part of this land is God calling us to?' We felt it was specifically the West End of San Antonio. There are lots of specific geographical areas of need around the world – many in Ibiza, even more in Spain, hundreds in Europe and so many more further afield. But our boundaries became clear for us when God started to stir our hearts for Ibiza and they got more defined as we prayer walked and asked God to reveal his heart to us. When we were in San Antonio we felt alive, we felt at home, we felt born to be there. We knew it was the specific piece of the land that he wanted us to work in.

What's your land? Know your land. Know what you are called to. You may be called to a whole city but it may be more specific – a neighbourhood or simply a street there. Some people are called to a people group rather than a geographical area. But you need to know your land.

Then, because we had a really strong sense that this was our land, we started prophetically to place our feet all over the land – to say that wherever we put our feet, that was where we wanted God's kingdom to come. Our physical act became a prophetic gesture in preparation for a spiritual reality. I have lost count of how many times I have walked the land and said, 'Your kingdom come!'

Possessing the land can sound almost colonial – and a little arrogant. But it's never *my* land or *our* land – it's *God's* land, it's *his* earth. We are just his representatives here, asking for a shift in the spiritual and physical atmosphere of a land. I don't want this land for my rule, I don't want this land so I can impose my ideals of what Christianity should be like upon it. I want Christ's kingdom expressed in his way, in the way that is most conducive to change being wrought in the lives of the people of that specific piece of land.

This is not a crusade. This is about me, a servant, treading gently, walking lightly and humbling myself throughout the land, asking for my King's kingdom to be established in whatever way he chooses. It's about me making myself open to his will, responding to what he wants for the land and discovering his heart for the land as I walk it. Walking it with humility.

BLESSING NOT SELLING

It's probably better to talk about redeeming the land rather than possessing it. Just before we set off for Ibiza, we were introduced to Floyd McClung, who challenged Tracy and I to 'concentrate on blessing not selling'. His wise advice took root and so we were always very conscious of blessing the land. It shaped the way we prayed and the way that we approached the mission.

Know your land. Walk around your land. Ask for God's kingdom to come in your land.

We learned that we needed to pray with conviction and faith, trying to be more positive than negative, praying redemptive, optimistic prayers.

Prayers like this:

> God I do believe you love this place ...
> I do believe you love these people ...
> I do believe you want to bring change ...
> I do believe you want to save people ...
> I do believe you can change people ...
> I do believe you can change this town ...

Those kinds of prayers.

REMINDING OURSELVES

It's easy to lose sight of who God is, looking at the task or challenge ahead and thinking 'It's too big!' But that's what we need to try to grasp: who God is, the power and authority that he has, and the passion that he has for people.

As we walked around and declared our faith in God, declared our confidence in his love and power – as we started to make these kinds of positive prayer statements – our faith grew and we began to understand God's power and passion more. We began to see how the spiritual darkness over San Antonio could be pushed back so that the light of God could burst through and restore the town to the beautiful place it was always intended to be. It is always better to focus on light rather than darkness.

In Matthew 16 there is a record of a conversation between Jesus and his disciples. Jesus asked them who people around are saying that he is, and then challenged them directly, "'But what about you?" he asked. "Who do you say I am?" Simon Peter answered, "You are the Messiah, the Son of the living God."' In response to this confident statement of faith, Jesus replies, "'... on this rock, I will build my church, and the gates of Hades will not overcome it'" (Matthew 16:15–16, 18).

We need to remember who God is, to remind ourselves and others too. There's something powerful about doing that. Hebrews 11:1 tells us, 'Now faith is confidence in what we hope for and assurance about what we do not see'. We needed to become confident of what we hoped for and sure of what we didn't see, and speak it out with conviction! It was a way of reminding ourselves, keeping us focussed and not allowing us to forget that this was all about what God could do.

por fe

God was teaching us how he wanted us to pray in this setting and we felt that he was telling us to pray redemptive prayers. Given all that had been reported about San Antonio, it would have been easy to pray prayers asking God to bring down, put a stop to, banish and destroy things that seemed to lead people into ways that were contrary to God's ways.

One day God reminded us of the story of Nineveh, a town that he had threatened to destroy because of their wickedness, and how when the people heard his message through Jonah, they changed their ways, causing God to show mercy and spare them. With the 'Sodom and Gomorrah' allegation still ringing in our ears, we prayed that San Antonio would be a Nineveh, not a Sodom and Gomorrah. We developed a new narrative for how we prayed and how we framed our prayers. It was a redemptive narrative, one that held on to the fact that on hearing the message, Nineveh turned and repented. We quickly dropped all references to Ibiza being Sodom and Gomorrah, and for us it became a 'Nineveh'.

In addition to that, we felt compelled to ask God to redeem the things that he had created, calling out the good that he intended through music, dance, pleasure, sexual intimacy, alcohol, drugs. Imagining all of these things in their appropriate, God-intended setting, gave a different picture of what they could be.

These words from Matthew became important to us and shaped our prayers and the way we tried to speak and act:

> "Let me tell you why you are here. You're here to be salt-seasoning that brings out the God-flavors of this earth. If you lose your saltiness, how will people taste godliness? You've lost your usefulness and will end up in the garbage.

> "Here's another way to put it: You're here to be light, bringing out the God-colors in the world. God is not a secret to be kept. We're going public with this, as public as a city on a hill. If I make you light-bearers, you don't think I'm going to hide you under a bucket, do you? I'm putting you on a light stand. Now that I've put you there on a hilltop, on a light stand – shine! Keep open house; be generous with your lives. By opening up to others, you'll prompt people to open up with God, this generous Father in heaven."

> Matthew 5:13–16   (*The Message*)

We were stirred to pray in a way that was calling out the good that God intended, bringing out the God-colours and God-flavours, asking that what God has made would be redeemed. This did keep the whole process of persistent walking and praying a lot more hope-filled – it's the only way we could have kept going for all those years.

These early lessons in prayer stuck. Every two-week team since those early days has started their time in Ibiza with a prayer walk. For seven years, we prayer walked around San Antonio.

When we took the teams out we set out as a group, but then spread out in pairs, walking and talking quietly, not all shouting out and looking weird. We just blessed the city.

We'd stop at certain places: we'd pray at the port, the town council offices; we'd pray God's blessing on Café Mambo, Café del Mar and other Sunset Strip bars where people gathered night after night; we'd pray near the quiet little cove, designated 'Ket Cove' by seasonal workers; we'd pray for the local health centre and the staff facing the increased volume of patients in the summer months; we'd look up at the hills and remember Psalm 121; we'd pray around the bars and clubs; we'd pray in the areas where we would see prostitutes at work by night. We stopped at roundabouts and prayed about what came into the town. And it was good.

PRAYER PSYCHOLOGY

I am a great believer in prayer walking. The visual stimulus inspires your prayers. There is a theory that each of us prefer to process information in different ways. Some people process through sound, and you will often hear these people use phrases like 'That sounds good', or, 'I like the sound of that'. Visual people process by picturing things and they will often say, 'I can see how that would work', or, 'I'm struggling to picture it'. Some others will process by how something feels, they will say 'This feels right', or 'I have a bad feeling about this'.

I'm not sure how accurate the theory is, but the idea made me wonder if it could help us to pray. I respond better to visual stimuli and to feelings, so I am more comfortable when I can see something and when it feels right.

Walking can provide good stimuli for all three and make your prayer life a little more interesting.

Here's how we did it in a little more detail:

First, seeing the public buildings and places prompted prayer. We would walk past the police station and pray that they would act justly and fairly. Passing the health centre, we would ask God to give the medical staff patience and grace, particularly in the height of summer when they felt stretched to breaking point, asking God to keep calling them back to their caring hearts that had first drawn them to choose that career. At the local council offices, we would ask God for the officials to have wisdom to make good choices, and that truth would triumph over corruption. As we passed the schools, we would ask that God would be part of the young lives that were learning and growing up, and that the teachers would be a positive influence on their students.

Then there were entry points. God reminded us to pray at the roundabouts that marked the entry points to the town and we would pray about what came in and out. We did the same at the port, asking God to guide those working to catch drug smugglers, placing them in the right place at the right time.

Also at beauty spots, simply seeing God's creation prompted prayer. Strolling along the Sunset Strip area, we would think of the hundreds of people who would gather every night of the summer to watch the spectacular sunsets, and we would praise God that 'the heavens declare the glory of the risen Lord'. And we asked that, night after night, as the crowds would applaud the final moment of the sun sinking into the calm Mediterranean Sea, God would remind them that he was the Creator of this beauty. The tiny bay known as 'Ket Cove', a nightly gathering point for people to meet and take drugs together, was a reminder to us to ask God to protect those people from harm in spite of the choices they were making. Sparkling salt crystals on rocks by the sea would inspire us to pray that, just as the sea washing over the rocks left a salty deposit behind, we would be people who left a 'salty' God deposit in the places we travelled.

Finally, we prayed places where people came to enjoy themselves. As we walked through the West End, with its variety of bars and clubs, we would pray for safety and protection of tourists. We would ask God to give managers and owners the integrity to run a clean business, not selling alcohol to people who had clearly got to a certain level of inebriation and keeping their bars as free of drugs as was within their power. And we asked that God would reward them for it.

We prayed in so many different ways over the years – sometimes we sprinkled seeds or anointed places with oil, sometimes we prayed Bible verses over the town. We prayed in twos and threes and with our eyes open, like having a conversation with God about our town, And we kept on praying, week after week, year after year.

UNEXPECTED ANSWERS

On every prayer walk we would walk by a rocky beach just outside Café Mambo where people would sit and watch the sunset. The teams before us had always gone here and prayed, so it felt completely natural for us to continue to do so. We would sit on the rocks and look out to sea and pray. People have sat in this spot for years, watching the sunset while beautiful music is played from the bars behind. Our prayer as we walked by, or stopped and sat, was always that people would be touched by the beauty of creation. That as they watched the sun, they would realise that before the sun, God existed; that in all the beauty they would somehow be stirred to think about the Creator behind creation.

Then one day I had a message from a girl who had been sitting watching the sunset at Café Mambo, had become overwhelmed by the realisation that she needed God in her life – and then gave her life to Jesus![2] There was no one there, no evangelist preaching, just God speaking through creation. But I can't help but think that if a group of Christians go and pray in the same spot for fifteen years, that if they walk around that spot repeatedly asking the same thing of God each time, eventually stuff will happen.

Sometimes we would hear stories like that, of things happening, of 'coincidences' happening when or where we prayed.

---

[2] See Chapter 11, *Secret Histories*.

Other times God would just lead us to the right place. Like when he led us to our first permanent prayer room. It was above a kebab shop, right in the heart of San Antonio and exactly where we wanted to be.

We had been praying for ten months for premises, for a prayer room and an office. One day when we were out prayer walking, we were asking God for an ideal spot to be based. We stopped to grab some water at a little café when I noticed a '*Se Aquila*' ('To Let') sign in the window of an office on the first floor of a building opposite. (Just an aside here: it is important to look up. We sometimes had our heads down as we walked, but on all walks it's good to stop and look up, spiritually speaking, and this time I looked up physically as well.)

We saw the sign so we got through a metal gate and climbed up some stairs just above a kebab shop. It was a little smelly. As we peered through the windows we saw two square rooms completely empty and painted white. The thought that jumped instantly to my mind was that they looked like two blank canvases. There was a phone number in a window. We prayed about it some more, then gave them a call and tried to negotiate a little. Even though the office had been empty for two years they wouldn't drop their rent! We caved in and took it, so we had our first permanent prayer room in the centre of the West End.

The location was perfect, right above the street, like an upper room. We moved in and started praying in it straight away. We decorated the prayer room, got a leather settee and did our best to make it look stylish. The other room was our office.

We didn't stop prayer walking though.

KEEPING ON

Someone asked me how we kept it up, all this prayer walking, week after week.

There were probably good days and bad days, and it was easier in the summer, when the weather was lovely and when the new teams showed up.

But I couldn't say it was ever particularly hard. It was just a natural thing to do. We walked because we felt inadequate, because we were overwhelmed, because we depended on God. We never felt up to the task – we never once felt we had it all sussed. If you look at San Antonio, it needs God to show up, so badly – and there was just Tracy and I. We walked to get perspective. We walked because we wanted to see breakthrough.

SOME PRAYER WALKING POINTERS

- Know your land. Find out where God is calling you to, specifically, and focus on that.

- Remember who God is. Walk humbly, but pray confidently, asking for his kingdom to come.

- Prayer walk in twos and threes, and with your eyes open – naturally, as if having a conversation. Swap and regroup now and then.

- Avoid distraction – don't go shopping! But do allow your prayers to be guided by what you see.

- Pray for the public places, using your knowledge of them – justice in the police station, dedication in the schools, integrity in the council offices.

- Pray for entry points, roundabouts, etc.

- Pray positive redemptive prayers, ask God to bring out the 'God-colours' and 'God-flavours'.

- Pray Bible verses over your town or city – and pray God's word back to God.

- Use creative and prophetic expression. Plant seeds or anoint places with oil.

- Keep a written record.

- Keep praying. Be persistent!

DIRTY PLACES

DIRTY PLACES 4

We jump in the van and start to make our way back to our prayer room from the hospital. As we are driving along we find a guy, covered in puke, who has definitely had far too much to drink. The beautiful thing is that his friend is sitting in the puke with him! We park up and jog back to help them out and inevitably, carrying him back to the van, we get vomit smeared on us. We deal with it. Normally it's on people's arms so when they put their arm around your neck and walk with you, it transfers onto the back of your neck. At first it's slippery but in the intense Spanish heat it soon dries out. It's always easier if the people we find have a less drunk friend with them, so that was a relatively painless bit of action, just a little slimy and smelly!

After that we find another guy on his own, completely drunk and vomiting – so we put him in the van and take him on a short journey back to his hotel. By now I really am starting to smell!

And here I am, after three hours of this kind of mayhem. I feel beaten, beaten up – you know that sense of having taken an emotional hammering. I haven't got tears, just aches and tiredness in my bones, sweat on my body and a slight smell of dried-out vomit clinging to my clothes and skin. This is the cost of prayer and mission for me here in San Antonio.

In fact I am so tired I can't even be bothered to have a shower so I go to bed at six in the morning smelling of sweat and vomit. Not pleasant for Tracy but if I'm honest I don't care – just let me sleep. Anyway she will be up to do the school run in an hour, and hopefully won't notice that I stink. Please don't get me wrong – I don't feel sorry for myself. This is a choice I've made. I don't feel overcome with self-pity – just confronted with the ongoing thought that to love and keep loving will cost me.

This journey has moved on and now it's continually pushing me to new levels of tiredness, caffeine is very quickly becoming a close friend. Caffeine only works for a while though, and it doesn't really help you emotionally. But I'm guessing you knew that ...

MESS

The West End of San Antonio is a lot of fun. It isn't like Space, it's very different. It's not as stylish and far less international – it's very British. It's also less self-conscious, more light-hearted, a lot cheaper, and actually, because of my own working-class-ness, it is the part of Ibiza that I feel most comfortable in. It caters mainly for groups of younger people or people on a budget holiday and at one time was said to have more bars, pubs and clubs per square mile than anywhere else on the European continent. These bars open until four or six in the morning and many offer budget deals – buy one get one free, all you can drink in an hour for €15, that kind of thing.

Many people drink sensibly and generally enjoy their holiday. But others drink too much, or take too many drugs. Those were the ones we helped – people who were in a state of drunken confusion and had been left behind or lost by their friends, easy targets for robbery. People who can't remember the name of their hotel and certainly not how to get there, or vulnerable young women who were in serious danger of being raped. Often we would be astounded at the completely wasted state people could get in through alcohol and drug use – and astounded at how their friends would just leave them and go on in a group to party.

There are some lines from a Moby song that go round in my head when I think of our evenings in the West End of San Antonio. Lines about places and heartache and faces, about seeing so many dirty things that you wouldn't believe.

It's funny how God uses our weak points. I'm not good with mess or dirt. In fact I can't stand it. I don't have OCD but I can't sit in a room with someone eating cornflakes loudly. In fact I don't like eating breakfast with others, I could not take a bite out of someone else's chocolate bar for fear of a saliva swap, and I would never drink from someone else's drink in case of backwash. I'm a bit squeamish really. It might be from my time in prison. I'm sure a psychologist could help me but it's not the biggest issue I have had to work through and I manage it quite well. God knows this – he knows me – and yet, knowing this, knowing me, he sent me to a place where the streets had to be washed down every morning because of the amount of beer, vomit and urine on them.

But I know, and he knows, that I can't react in disgust when I'm helping someone, I have to react with love.

And yet even though I am naturally squeamish, I have never really reacted too badly to the mess when I'm actually out at night. Maybe it's because I'm the guy who likes to rush in, to save the day. I act first and think later. That *can* get me into lots of trouble, but in a situation when there is loads of mess you could say it's a strength. It isn't until afterwards that I think about what we have just done. Or maybe its because I've been given grace for this. But whatever it is, I know that he has given me everything I need to deal with it.

Probably the worst time was the night I got vomit actually *in* my mouth. All the way home I was just driving and spitting – *all* the way. Even though it was five in the morning when I got back, I poured myself a large single malt – someone had been to stay and brought us a bottle – and I held it in my mouth as long as I could, hoping that it would sterilise my mouth.

Someone – I think it might have been Winston Churchill – said, 'We are not judged by our actions but by our reactions'. We want to react in the right way to all the messiness that we see.

We cannot react in disgust when we see a broken generation covered in its own vomit. We cannot react with disgust when we see our generation take huge quantities of drugs. We cannot react with disgust when see a lonely generation have sex with as many partners as possible in some false search for intimacy. We have to react with love, with grace, with compassion.

We would sometimes stand and pray in a beautiful place looking out towards a huge rock called *Es Vedra*. It sits about a mile and a half out at sea and is incredibly imposing, vast, something that overwhelms and leaves you with a feeling of smallness and inadequacy. The state of our generation can be like that. But what I need to know, what I need assurance about, is that when I see the mess and get down in it, that it pushes the right button, that it prompts the right reaction.

I need to know that I will react with love. I need to know that I won't react with disgust or judgmentalism or impatience. I do get overloaded sometimes, but if the journey I am on is one of love, one of expressing God's love, surely he will give me all I need to live this life. The vastness of the problem can only be matched by the vastness of God's love, of which the apostle Paul says:

> For this reason I kneel before the Father, from whom every family in heaven and on earth derives its name. I pray that out of his glorious riches he may strengthen you with power through his Spirit in your inner being, so that Christ may dwell in your hearts through faith. And I pray that you, being rooted and established in love, may have power, together with all the Lord's holy people, to grasp how wide and long and high and deep is the love of Christ, and to know this love that surpasses knowledge – that you may be filled to the measure of all the fullness of God.
>
> Now to him who is able to do immeasurably more than all we ask or imagine, according to his power that is at work within us, to him be glory in the church and in Christ Jesus throughout all generations, for ever and ever! Amen.
>
> Ephesians 3:14–21

I need to be 'rooted and established in love' – in the vastness of this love – if I am going to deal with the mess and pain that is out there. I need to express his love, a love that surpasses all knowledge. Think about it: what is knowledge? Knowledge is knowing. Knowledge is what we know we know, what we can define, what we can say with certainty we understand. Knowledge is our questions answered. Yet here we have a love that goes beyond that!

That's fantastic – a love that surpasses my questions, even my How? Why? Where? When? An unexplainable love. A love beyond knowledge, a long, high, deep love. As a child I used to sing, 'Jesus' love is very wonderful ... So high you can't get over it, so low you can can't get under it, so wide you can't get around it'. I love this song. I want to live my life expressing the sentiment of this song.

There were times when I didn't know how to process all we saw and other times when it was so busy it all just blurred into one and I didn't get time to process any of it. You just had to get on with it and maybe process it later – or maybe just have a beer and relax later. I didn't feel overloaded by it, more a sense of numbness. Numb at the wave of mess we witnessed every night we were out.

We put ourselves in the position of finding the mess so we were asking for it, but that didn't make it easy. And isn't that what we are called to do? If we are meant to express love, shouldn't we go and put ourselves in the positions and places where love needs most to be expressed? Isn't it right for us to seek out this messiness? This is where the rubber really hits the road in prayer and mission, where God calls our bluff in prayer, calls us out into mission. If love drives us, it will lead us to messy, dirty places. That might not always be physical mess – there are many places where wonderful smiles and great clothes hide a pile of messiness. However for us in Ibiza the mess was often physical, and through prayer we learned how to love in it. We need to learn how to love in whatever situation we are in.

I remember being at a gathering called *Remix* in 1996. After one of the main sessions the two guys who had been speaking, Roger Ellis and Roger Mitchell, just got two big bags of soil and threw them into the crowd. Their challenge was that God was calling us to go – and that if we did take up that challenge it would mean that we ended up with dirty hands. That if were truly going to bring light to darkness there would be mess involved – we would have to get our hands dirty. As a prophetic response we had to dig our hands into the soil. I remember clambering towards the bag of soil with hundreds of other people and plunging my hands deep into the dirt, and they came out dirty and messed up. Little did I know that one day this prophetic symbolism would become a reality in my own life.

Maybe in reading some of our stories about getting involved in mess, you've thought, 'I could never do that', or even, 'If they are going to get themselves into such a state, they should deal with the consequences'. I do believe that God gave us grace (and tough gag reflexes) in these situations. But we would also remind ourselves that this was someone's daughter, someone's son – and wouldn't we be grateful to think that if our girls, our sons were ever in such a mess, someone might just take the time to help them?

Think of a sixteen-year-old girl you know, someone from your friendship circle, church or family. If you saw her vomiting, drunk and in a mess, you would help her, and clean her up. You would see through the mess because you knew her. God knows every one of us, so he will always see through the mess. He knows us intimately.

The Psalmist puts it like this:

> You have searched me, Lord,
>   and you know me.
>
> You know when I sit and when I rise;
>   you perceive my thoughts from afar.
>
> You discern my going out and my lying down;
>   you are familiar with all my ways...
>
> For you created my inmost being;
>   you knit me together in my mother's womb.
>
> I praise you because I am fearfully and wonderfully made;
>   your works are wonderful,
>   I know that full well.
>
> My frame was not hidden from you
>   when I was made in the secret place,
>   when I was woven together in the depths of the earth.
>
> Your eyes saw my unformed body;
>   all the days ordained for me were written in your book
>   before one of them came to be.
>
> Psalm 139:1–3, 13–16

JUDGE NOT ...

We often find it hard to explain why a Christian charity would choose to work somewhere like San Antonio. This work is not easy to justify

– it's not like building schools in Africa, feeding orphans or helping the homeless. This is working with people who have deliberately set out to have a lot to drink, embrace casual sexual encounters or to take drugs. This is a generation on a mission: the mission is to party hard, live for the moment, and deal with the consequences later!

Obviously there is more to it than that: there are lots of people who are just looking for a temporary escape from a whole variety of problems and situations. But wouldn't it be better to send Christian missionaries to people who really deserve assistance, who genuinely need help, whose tough situations come about through circumstances outside of their control? Wouldn't it be better to head towards an area where people are actually calling out for help and are glad to see you when you turn up?

The people we were meeting weren't intentionally looking for God, but before we moved to Ibiza, we had really felt led to this verse:

> I was found by those who did not seek me;
>   I revealed myself to those who did not ask for me.
>
> Romans 10:20

This was always our hope and our prayer.

Loving the broken will cost you, and at times will push all the wrong buttons. In fact it's harder when people don't actually see themselves as broken because the god of this age has blinded their minds (2 Corinthians 4:4). So there you are, trying to love and help them, when they think they are doing fine!

Yet we are called to love – not just to love when it's easy or deserved or appreciated, but to love at *all* times, in all ways, regardless of the cost.

Working amongst all this messiness can provoke a reaction, a prejudicial attitude. Why would someone drink that much? Who would be stupid enough to take so many drugs? Why would someone's friends leave him or her alone on the streets? It can push all the wrong buttons.

I sometimes struggle with feelings of annoyance towards people who get in a mess – it's judgmentalism. The very same that happens at the school gates when people make different lifestyle choices to us, when they spend their money on a car or holiday we don't think fits their wage bracket, when they allow their child to do stuff we wouldn't allow ours to do ... In fact it's probably easier to move a half-naked, semi-comatose girl to safety than it is to deal with the fact that the unemployed guy across the road has just bought a 50-inch plasma screen.

I am certainly no 'Brother Theresa' (in the words of the late Brennan Manning). There are plenty of times when I don't get it right. If we are called to prayer and mission, buttons will be pushed, we will be stretched, and we won't always deal with it very well.

On one particularly messy evening, we had just taken a guy who had drunk far too much vodka home. Then we got a call out to help a really large girl home. Heavy, drunk people are really hard to move. If there are male volunteers on hand, it tends to be they who do the lifting – but if it's a girl that needs lifting it gets tricky: you don't quite know where to put your hands.

Two of our volunteers, Helen and Bethany, spent ages with this girl. They had been looking after her and her friend for an hour before Bruce and I turned up in the van. We eventually bundled them into our van, then drove them about three miles to their hotel. When we got to the hotel the younger, more sober girl was extremely rude to the very helpful hotel staff. I tried to calm her and asked her to quietly get into the lift and go to her room. She then told me to 'f**k off'. I politely pointed out what we had just tried to do for her but she just stormed off swearing.

Bethany went after her as she drunkenly stumbled up the stairs – the last thing we wanted was for her to fall down and hurt herself. But the girl snapped. She turned and took one of her shoes off and used it to slap Bethany on her face and her back and then ran off. This girl was only 16! It was horrible. I was so furious, everything in me wanted to go and smack this girl, which I know is not very godly. The guy on reception was also very angry – I thought he was going to kill her. But there was nothing we could do. We had dropped them with their parents and they were safe, so we left them.

I was annoyed with myself because I'd reacted to the drunk girl by trying to put her right, by telling her what we had done for her to try to make her grateful. I think it made her more angry, which in turn may have contributed to Bethany getting a slap. I was also angry with myself for letting Bethany run after her and backing off myself. And I was angry with the girl.

My anger is initially verbal, but it soon turns into an inner dialogue. An inner rant. My mind becomes full of thoughts of what I would like to do and say, my heart is pounding as I imagine going back the next day and humiliating this girl into an apology in front of her parents. I'm sinning and I am enjoying the sin, it's feeding some monster within me. Even if I don't go back and prove my superior position, the self-righteous attitude, which is bordering on a revenge fantasy, is running rampant.

All the wrong buttons had been pushed. I hadn't acted on them but I knew something in me was just a little off. We had wanted a happy ending, thanks maybe, praise even. But all we had got was a slap and a few swear words. To say it left a bad taste in our mouths was an understatement.

We then had the opportunity to get back into the prayer room for a few minutes, a moment to breathe in. I probably ran a few verses through my mind, verses that help me when I am stressed, 'Be still before the Lord and wait patiently for him' (Psalm 37:7), or 'Be still, and know that I am God' (Psalm 46:10).

Sometimes sitting silently helps. It helped me then. I love this old verse from a hymn:

> Sacred silence! Thou that art
> Floodgate of the deeper heart,
> Offspring of a heavenly kind;
> Frost o' the mouth, and thaw o' the mind
>
> *Richard Flecknoe*

Sitting in a prayer room silently can thaw out the mind, remove the hard frosty edges that incidents like this can put on us.

I calmed myself and started to ask, 'How can I be like this? I am an object of mercy who should have known wrath!' In the heat of the moment I had forgotten just how much I was loved, how often I had figuratively slapped God in the face or sworn at him – and yet he goes on loving me, he goes on loving me, he goes on loving me, he goes on loving me.

I had forgotten the lesson I learned that day in Space, about God loving those girls every bit as much as he loves me, as much as he loves my family.

When we spend time in the place of prayer, we begin to learn to love more and judge less.

I want to write about how of course God wants people's behaviour to change and they need to be confronted with their misdeeds. But that would be missing the point of this chapter. First he wants *my* behaviour to change! He goes on loving me. I am pretty sure I must do everything possible to press the wrong buttons in God all the time – but he goes on loving me. It's that love that brings change, not confrontation.

Anyone who has become a Christian recently will tell you they became aware of the love first, then the change happened. John 3:16 became real to them. Prayer should always bring us back to love.

Rules don't love people. People love people.

That night, we only had a few moments to get our hearts back on track – we had to drive on and pick up another girl who had got totally wasted and take her home. She and her friend were lovely girls and very grateful. More often than not people are actually looking to be helped and when we offer the appropriate help, they respond with gratitude – sometimes we just need to be brave enough to offer.

Over the years we had far more positive reactions than negative ones and these next two girls were just a bit lost, a bit drunk and very happy to be helped. Yet we had shown them the same love we had shown to the other two. The same love can provoke different responses.

It's difficult when people don't appreciate your help, don't realise they need it. And situations can get so dangerous. My blog tells me that earlier that same night ...

> We were praying in the prayer room when the phone rang. A friendly bar worker called us out to a nearby bar, to help a young man who had been beaten up by another drunken holidaymaker. When we arrived, what struck me was how young this guy was. As often with alcohol, it's hard to get an accurate picture of what had

gone on, but he was bleeding from a head wound and needed to be looked at. He wasn't in a bad enough way for San Antonio's already overstretched ambulance service and there was no way a taxi driver was going to take someone who was bleeding like that. So we took the young guy to hospital in our Vomit Van and left him there. We always operate in twos and if it ever looks like we can't handle it, we call an ambulance or the police. Tonight this guy was OK, he was talking, coherent and relatively with it, the hospital is only 4 minutes away. We predominantly deal with what I could only call the walking wounded, not always physically wounded but also the emotionally wounded. Well, the physically wounded guy soon sobers up, gets stitched up and makes his way home.

Later, at a hotel we had a disturbing conversation with a traumatised hotel porter. A 19-year-old holidaymaker had died the previous evening in his hotel from a drink or drugs over-dose. He was broken and upset – all we could do was listen. Think about it, he's a hotel porter. His job is to hand people their keys and help them with their luggage – not deal with them dying. In the face of the emotionally wounded, sometimes all we can do is listen. There are tears in his eyes and he won't let us take the drunk up to his room but makes us leave him in reception where he can keep a watchful and caring eye on him.

At the end of that night – after eight hours of madness, of helping grateful girls and ungrateful ones, of helping young guys who'd been beaten up and hotel staff who'd been traumatised, guys who were unable to stand, guys whose trousers wouldn't stay up, guys who forgot their hotel or their shoes – we called it a night and came home. I sat in a daze trying to process all that had happened. I wasn't depressed – more distressed. I was sad and battered but alive and happy. This is fulfilling, frustrating, energising and wearying work. Prayer and mission is like this – it's a roller coaster.

I came to prefer quiet nights on the street and busy days in the centre. It is never very pleasant to see people in such a mess.

But we helped where we could and at the end of each night we knew that those people were sleeping safely, which is kind of satisfying.

I often think about the words Jesus once said: 'I tell you the truth, whatever you did for one of the least of these brothers of mine, you did for me.' This is like worship. It's that beautiful moment when, in the midst of serving others, God draws near to you. It's like a lovely act of worship – you lift up praise to him by serving the needy and broken and somehow he pours something into you.

Prayer will lead you out – you may not know what to do, but still you do what you can. Learning that we shouldn't stand back but that we need to get involved is the most beautiful act of worship we can perform.

Paul sums it up rather nicely in Romans 12, and *The Message* version is great. It could well be worth reading or even memorising this as an aid to prayer and mission:

> ... if you're called to give aid to people in distress, keep your eyes open and be quick to respond; if you work with the disadvantaged, don't let yourself get irritated with them or depressed by them. Keep a smile on your face.
>
> Love from the center of who you are; don't fake it. Run for dear life from evil; hold on for dear life to good. Be good friends who love deeply; practice playing second fiddle.
>
> Don't burn out; keep yourselves fueled and aflame. Be alert servants of the Master, cheerfully expectant. Don't quit in hard times; pray all the harder. Help needy Christians; be inventive in hospitality.
>
> Bless your enemies; no cursing under your breath. Laugh with your happy friends when they're happy; share tears when they're down. Get along with each other; don't be stuck-up. Make friends with nobodies; don't be the great some-body.
>
> Don't hit back; discover beauty in everyone. If you've got it in you, get along with everybody. Don't insist on getting even; that's not for you to do. "I'll do the judging," says God. "I'll take care of it."

Our Scriptures tell us that if you see your enemy hungry, go buy that person lunch, or if he's thirsty, get him a drink. Your generosity will surprise him with goodness. Don't let evil get the best of you; get the best of evil by doing good.

Romans 12:8–21   (*The Message*)

Let's try to see past the mess, let's get our hands dirty, and let's get the better of evil by doing good.

PRAYER ROOMS

PRAYER ROOMS

5

We took a friend to the airport last night. He had been working in various bars over the summer and slowly got sucked in to drinking more and more heavily. It was pretty scary to see him deteriorate over the summer just from alcohol abuse. He was thin, he wasn't always clean, his hands shook and he would occasionally break down in tears when he had sudden moments of recognising his own state.

Our team helped him. He was able to come in and shower in our centre, use the phone, sort out his emails and eventually get someone to pay for his flight home. He was in such a muddle. So we took him to the airport, helped him get his bags checked in and made sure he got through security. We have prayed for him and with him a lot over the last few weeks and the night before he left we prayed with him once again.

He doesn't want to come back. Unfortunately for him San Antonio has chewed him up and spat him out. So many workers cope admirably here, but occasionally you get people who have a drinking background or have not properly researched how hard it is to get a great job here and they struggle.

When our friend got in the car on his last night to go to the airport, he said, 'At last, I feel safe'. He obviously had never seen my driving, but I knew what he meant.

SANCTUARY

Isn't this what church, the community of Christ, is meant to do – provide safety, refuge and help for the broken, scared and vulnerable?

In the 1600s Ibiza was subject to attacks by bands of marauding pirates. The churches responded by building fortifications, so that when the pirates attacked, the villagers could run into the church and hide there as a place of refuge and sanctuary. The church in San Antonio is one of the best examples of this type of architecture. They even had cannons on the roof to fight the pirates off. This protection was not just passive, providing a place to hide. It was also actively aggressive, with the means to fire on the attackers and hurt them back.

I like that picture of church.

When we moved into the centre, we tried to recapture some of that ancient spirit, of the church building as sanctuary, a place of safety, a shelter. That was our heart for a permanent prayer room in Ibiza. We wanted people to come into contact with our community and say, 'At last, I feel safe'.

We wanted a prayer room as a place of sanctuary, and it happened. People who were very down on their luck or having a particularly bad moment used our prayer room. We prayed with people in it, some just sat in there for a while, some people came down from drugs in it, we counselled people in it. It was and is a place of sanctuary.

Prayer rooms are spaces where people can feel safe. The psalmist wrote:

> One thing I ask from the Lord,
>   this only do I seek:
> that I may dwell in the house of the Lord
>   all the days of my life,
> to gaze on the beauty of the Lord
>   and to seek him in his temple.
> For in the day of trouble
>   he will keep me safe in his dwelling;
> he will hide me in the shelter of his sacred tent
>   and set me high upon a rock.
>
> Psalm 27:4–5

People would often literally feel like they were being hidden 'in the shelter of his sacred tent'. Hidden from the mayhem, the chaos, the heat, the pressure to keep the image going, the need to perform, the need to act like they had it all together. They could hide from it all and feel safe in his presence, in this space we had created.

But they are also more than just safe places.

HEAVEN TOUCHING EARTH

In 24-7 Prayer we love prayer rooms. They are a great way to facilitate prayer – weeks of prayer, prayer rhythms, or a place to retreat to and meet with God. Most prayer rooms are not permanent – they are set up for a week in all manner of places.

They actually became places of encounter. Our experience in Ibiza was that people would walk in who had no Christian or church background and say, 'It feels different in here' or, 'It feels so peaceful in here'. As a good old-fashioned Protestant, I was surprised by the fact that the room itself carried a special feel.

But then the place where we meet God *is* special. It is not to be taken for granted, not to be messed with. In the Old Testament, this was well understood. Next to the burning bush, Moses was told to take off his shoes as he was standing on holy ground. Mount Sinai became a holy mountain – the people were told not to go near it, not to touch it, or they would die. Uzzah was struck down simply for stretching out a hand to steady the Ark of the Covenant. And in the Temple, there was one part, the holiest of holies, where the priest could only go in once a year.

Since Jesus' death and resurrection, that has changed. Jesus told the woman at the well that a time was coming when it wouldn't be about where we worshipped, but that we will worship 'in the Spirit and in truth' (John 4:23). Nevertheless Jesus himself would go out onto the mountainside to pray. And places where people pray a lot – where people meet with God – often take on a very special atmosphere. The Celts called these places 'thin places'. What they meant by that was a place where the 'divide' between heaven and earth seemed to be particularly thin. Where heaven almost touches earth. When we first painted the prayer room, it took about four coats of paint to get it right – layer upon layer of paint changed the look of the room and I wonder if it is like that – that layers upon layers of prayers in a place change the feel?

We have found in 24-7 Prayer that the most ordinary of places – a room in an office block, a classroom, a bedroom in the YMCA – these places can take on a very special atmosphere when people have been praying in there. When people have been crying out to God, night and day, writing their prayers on a wall, hanging them on a line, writing them in a book, singing their praise.

I once helped to start a week of prayer in the Persian Gulf. This is what one of the team wrote:

> We hung lining paper round the walls, and when we finished the room was like a blank canvas. We didn't know if people would realise they could write their prayers on the walls. How wrong we were. At the end of the first week the walls of the room had become completely covered with prayers, drawings and scripture. Everyone wanted to continue for another week, but there was no more space for people to write on the walls. We didn't want to take any prayers down, so we covered them with another layer of lining paper – by the end of the three weeks, there were three layers of lining paper, prayer was layered on prayer, all around that room.
>
> Later, in the same prayer room, in the week before Easter, a group of women began to read the end of Mark's Gospel together. They were unable to read the words of the humiliation of Jesus without choking up in tears. These are holy moments.[1]

In another prayer room, in a Nissen hut in Scotland, one of the team described it like this:

> I welcomed a sensible, conservative, middle-aged woman into the prayer room. She had stoutly opposed the very idea of a week of prayer in their church. When

---

[1]   S J Heald, Well of Life Prayer Room, April 2011.

> she walked over the threshold she was simply overcome by tears. She spent an hour just kneeling, weeping at the cross.
>
> That same week a new Christian, who had been baptised the day before, was praying in the prayer room and found a new language just bubbling up as she prayed on her own. She was speaking in tongues for the very first time.[2]

Our 24-7 Prayer communities have always developed permanent prayer spaces. By a 'permanent' prayer space we don't mean a place were we permanently pray, disengaging from the world, but a place that is continually available to facilitate rhythms of prayer for communities engaged in prayer and mission. These often seem to become 'thin places', for a while or for longer.

Do all missional communities need a prayer room? I think that the answer is yes, wherever possible. If you are going to do mission and prayer, you need a place to pray, to withdraw and spend time with the Lord. Most churches or communities need a space set aside that they can dedicate to prayer.

BUILDING OUR PRAYER ROOM

After we signed the lease on the centre, we moved in and decorated. We decided that if we were going to do a prayer room, a space that facilitated a connection with the Lord, we needed to do it well, and we needed to invest a bit of time and money. The 'shabby chic' approach is all very well but if it's not done well, it tends to look more shabby than chic! Someone donated a sofa but we had to throw it away as it was full of fleas. So we painted the walls white, raised some money and bought a leather sofa, some other stylish furniture, nice tables, great pictures and a lava lamp, kept to accents of red and burnt orange and generally tried to make it tasteful.

---

[2] S J Heald, Auchterarder Week of Prayer, May 2008.

We didn't want it to look typically Christian, and we didn't want any prayer room clichés – no giant waves crashing over you, nothing too busy. We just wanted to dress the room nicely, to create a safe quiet place in the midst of a chaotic and noisy environment.

We did put a few creative resources in there – books for people to write and draw in, and some prayer stations that we would change now and then – pebbles to put in bowls of water, a shredder to shred your prayers of repentance and confession, bottles hanging from the ceiling for people to put 'message in a bottle' private prayers in – all that sort of stuff.

We did have a prayer wall. Out on the street we found people liked to fill in a prayer request card. So we put all the prayer cards up on the wall and worked out a system: once we had prayed for someone's prayer request, we put a green dot on it so that we knew and they knew it had been prayed for. By the end of our first summer we had about a thousand of these prayer requests posted on the wall.

But we resisted the temptation to make a notice board area displaying all our activities – we wanted to make the space less about doing and more about being. We didn't want to encourage shopping list praying: we wanted a place of reflection, interaction and peace.

We started praying there immediately. Our prayer room was so central to the heart and rhythm of prayer that we eventually organised the work around it.

BREATHING IN, BREATHING OUT

Our prayer pattern or rhythm developed through a kind of trial and error basis – but once we got in the flow, it worked really well.

In our first season we would send almost our whole team out every night, leaving just one or two people to stay back and pray, swapping over every hour. We'd just ask, 'Who wants to go out?' Sometimes everyone wanted to go out, no-one wanted to pray and stay in. One night I was the only one left in and everyone else had gone out. And I fell asleep. Then I heard the door go, I quickly sat up and, because I was half-asleep and couldn't quite string a prayerful sentence together, pretended to be praying in tongues. Not the greatest bit of prayer cover I have ever provided!

Towards the middle of that first summer I lost my confidence – I ended up saying, night after night, 'Don't worry, you guys go out, and I'll stay in'. I was pretending that I had it all covered, that I would stay back, like the great prayer warrior, and make intercession for the teams while they went out to proclaim the good news of the Kingdom! I did pray while the team were out – but it wasn't really because I was a fantastic intercessor. I had become tired of the late nights. I had become intimidated by the constant darkness, and had even been overwhelmed by the sheer numbers and chaos of it all. I had started to feel the pressure and was beginning to retreat. I would sit quietly in the prayer room and sometimes even just doze off.

People had heard stories about the work of the short-term teams, stories of healings, stories of God working. They arrived with high expectations and I started to take responsibility for those expectations rather than giving them to God. And, if I'm honest, the more that people talked and got excited, the more convinced I was that we wouldn't meet expectations. I allowed the darkness to get bigger. It took over and caused me to retreat into the prayer room.

I don't think I'm alone in retreating into legitimate spiritual activity to get out of connecting with the real world. Maybe I was just clinging on to my own melting iceberg ...

Then God gently started to remind me of my calling – that 'If God is for us, who could be against us?' (Romans 8:31). That 'greater is he that is in you than he that is in the world' (1 John 4:4 KJV). It was gentle, not rousing. Just gentle Bible verses starting to bring reassurance.

Then one day I watched the third *Lord of the Rings* movie, *Return of the King*, with my boys. When King Theodon rallies the troops to save the people of Minas Tirith, just before they charge into battle, he cries out, 'Fear No Darkness!' That line rang in my ears like a gentle noise from heaven. It felt as if God himself said those words directly to me. 'Fear no darkness!' God spoke and I believed him.

(Actually, a few weeks ago I was catching a train to London and Bernard Hill, the actor who plays Theodon, got on and sat next to me. I wanted to thank him for his words of encouragement during a hard spiritual time, or maybe just take a sneaky photo, but I bottled it and sat in awe as I cast my mind back to the time that this once fearsome king had inspired me to fear no darkness – whilst we both sat on the 8.19 to Liverpool Street.)

That summer in Ibiza, as I further pondered my loss of confidence, I also remembered that it was said of the great Carthaginian general, Hannibal, that he would never ask of his men anything he wasn't willing to do himself. This challenged me on the level of being a leader who practices what he preaches.

I also realised that I was exhausted. Sometimes I think we can mistake an attack of the enemy for just plain tiredness. The SAS say, 'Sleep is a weapon'. I believe that. Sometimes it's the darkness fighting back; but sometimes we are just tired. So, over a period of a few weeks, a combination of Biblical encounters, movie pep talks and a good rest got me back to a better place. I think most of the time, when we lose our mojo, it's a mixture of pressure, wrong thinking, demonic attack and yes, sometimes, just plain tiredness that does it.

It took me about a month to get it back.

We also started to realise that on the summer teams we would get a mixture of personality types – everybody is different. Some prefer to stay in and others want to go out. We'd usually expect at least one really bouncy, enthusiastic, talkative person, the type who just wanted to get out there. There would also be a cool, calm and collected type, who was usually nervous underneath. And then there were the absolutely petrified people.

There was one particularly challenging night with a two-week team that wanted to be out all the time, which left our longer term team, who were trying to form the lasting relationships, having to be in and praying. And we realised that to just allow Bouncy Enthusiasm to go out on the street and Absolutely Petrified to stay in and pray didn't reflect what we were trying to do – we couldn't have a mentality creeping in that almost said, 'I pray, you reach out' or, 'I reach out, you pray'. We all needed to do both.

It all began to add up: we realised we had to change something.

So we implemented some practical structures: in for an hour, out for an hour. That was the rhythm. We would divide the team in two: half would go out on the street, the other half would stay in the prayer room and pray. We would swap in and out. It was to give everyone a healthy rhythm, to give everyone a chance to be involved. And it didn't allow anyone to get out of anything.

It was also to stop me from bottling it.

Pete Greig wrote a lovely chapter in Andy Freeman's book *Punk Monk* on the ancient art of breathing. He says this: 'Life begins by breathing in, but unless we breathe out, we die! The primary call, as we have seen, is to withdraw in prayer, but we are also commanded to go out from that place of intimacy in order to advance the kingdom of heaven.'[3]

Our work out on the streets at night in Ibiza was like a rhythm of breathing. We'd spend an hour in the prayer room, 'breathing' God in and then an hour walking the streets, 'breathing' him out. In and out. That became the rhythm of our work.

Pete goes on to say:

> We must not fail to inhale the breath of God (by which we were created and without which we die) through disciplined prayer and meditation upon Scripture. And having inhaled God's breath, we may breathe out his life in loving mission, acts of mercy, celebratory worship and generous hospitality.
>
> Balance the inward breath of prayer with the outward breath of social engagement.

So none of what we do out on the street happens without prayer in the room or in private. But that time in the prayer room also propels us out. Breathing in, breathing out.

Sometimes it was a little less, sometimes a little more than an hour. A team might get caught up doing something or helping someone so they would be late. But we would always ask that pairs phone and check in on the hour, and say 'We're just with someone, we're on our way'. That way we knew they were safe. But an hour in and an hour out was the pattern – it was not an optional extra and it worked.

Some would be unhappy with this rhythm: because we all like great stories, and real good God connections were happening out on

---

[3] *Punk Monk: New Monasticism and the Ancient Art of Breathing,* Andy Freeman and Pete Greig, Survivor, Eastbourne (2007).

the street – people were being prayed for, conversations were being had that were mind blowing – you could feel like you had missed out because you were in the room praying. But we would say to teams, 'It is not what you have done individually but what you have done as a team'.

We made sure that, at handover, the team coming in would tell the stories of what they'd seen, and who they had helped, to the prayer team before they then went out. You had to accept that, although you wouldn't know every story or be physically involved in every story, your prayers contributed to every story. We would also encourage those praying to record some of the significant prayers or thoughts coming out of their hour of prayer, so that the returning pairs could flow into what had already been prayed. Breathing in, breathing out.

There were still some nights where something major happened, and someone just wouldn't get out – they would have to suck it up and stay in for several hours. And there were times when the prayer room did feel like an emergency room – we weren't sending police cars or ambulances, we were sending prayers. We'd get instructions like, 'OK, you guys pray about where her hotel is, then call us back'. We would just pray that they found the hotel and, more often than not, they would. There would be constant communication between the team out on the street and the team back in the room.

In the prayer room we prayed aloud. Some people, the contemplatives, weren't always comfortable with that. But we'd say, 'There is lots of time for contemplation'. Praying at night is different to praying in the day – it is easy to drift into sleep. And if people only pray in their heads, no-one can join in or agree. It was a bit of a bugbear of mine, people who wouldn't pray out loud. Praying out loud is Biblical. So we'd give them a little prayer guide. At one point we even gave targets: we'd say, 'When we are praying, we need four to five verbal contributions per hour, per person'. Anyone from a foreign country could pray in their own language, but then give a brief synopsis.

Sometimes we would get specific pictures whilst praying. Someone would get a picture of, say, a guy in a red jumper – and then meet a guy in a red jumper. It would be just the person they had pictured and would inevitably lead to a quite significant God encounter. Breathing in, breathing out.

At times we would focus our prayers on a particular group, or be led to pray for them. The patterns were remarkable. We might be praying for prodigals – and then would find ourselves out on the street and bumping into backslidden people. One time we had been praying like that before we went out and met someone who had been booted out of church when she was seventeen. She used to be a Sunday school teacher, but was told she could no longer teach Sunday school because she had fallen pregnant but wasn't married, and they had asked her to leave. She said, 'Pray for my son, he's a good boy, he is. Don't pray for me. I don't deserve your prayers'.

Just before going out, Tracy had been reminded of a verse in John, 'God didn't go to all the trouble of sending his Son merely to point an accusing finger, telling the world how bad it was. He came to help, to put the world right again' (John 3:17 *The Message*). Tracy showed her this verse, gave her the Bible and bookmarked that specific verse for her. She was then able to hold her hand, pray with her, encourage her.

On another occasion, a prayer time had been focused on praying for people who had real issues of low self-esteem and we had been drawn to the verses in Psalm 139 that remind us that God saw us and formed us, before we were even born or seen by human eyes. We prayed that individuals would know that they were precious to God.

In the next hour, Tracy listened to one guy's heartbreaking story of how he had almost died as a baby, had his leg amputated following a road accident at the age of around five, had battled with his sexuality and the difficulty of coming out, had attempted suicide and had arrived at the conclusion that he was not meant to be alive. I think that God had dropped that psalm into Tracy's mind in order that she could convey God's heart for this lad – who had been through such trauma – to pray for him and encourage him.

WELCOMING PEOPLE IN

But in the prayer room, in those early days, it was only us and our teams who used it. We would ask people, 'Do you want to come to the prayer room?' and they would look at us as though we were strange. We realised that we needed something more, a reason for people to come to us, another service we could offer, another point of connection.

We went to Tenerife and saw a work that was similar to ours, and they had something called 'The Living Room'. They had amazing premises and we were a bit jealous. It was a place where workers came and hung out – they had a pool table, laptops, a games area. We saw that workers liked to be there. I told the team all about it – and we started praying for it.

Some larger premises came up. They seemed perfect, so we went and looked at them and thought they would be excellent. We all went to pray as a team. But on the way back, or the next day, a verse just dropped into my mind: 'What is that in your hand?' (Exodus 4:2). And we realised that God was saying to us that we were to use fully what he had given us first.

We began to ask ourselves, 'What have we got in our hands?' and how we could fully use what we had. And we asked ourselves, 'What do people need, when they come on holiday?' We didn't want to start a café or sell anything because that would take business from the locals. But we realised the workers needed to be in touch with home, they needed Internet. So the next season we installed free Internet.

Then they came. It was somewhere for the workers to chill out on their afternoons off. Eventually we had to start manning the centre from four till eight every afternoon. It even became a bit crowded – people would be sitting outside, on the steps above the kebab shop, *El Rey de Donor*, King of Kebabs. There was no toilet so we used the kebab shop toilet. It wasn't ideal and the owner got a bit fed up – but then we let him use the Internet and encouraged all our people to buy kebabs and he was much happier.

After a couple of summers we really had outgrown our offices and prayer room. We were using what we had to the fullest possible extent. Winston Churchill said, 'At first we shape our buildings, then our buildings shape us'. Once you have a permanent prayer space in place, it will begin to shape you and your community. It was time to move, to allow the work to grow.

Early the following year the premises we'd seen before came up for rent again, and we took them. They were off a little street at ground level, and had a shop front with glass doors that you could open wide.

It provided potential for a prayer room as well as a drop-in centre for workers. We decorated it, built a dividing wall and made a prayer room. We made a long workbench for the computers, bought a plasma screen, an X-Box, a Wii, a pool table and some leather settees. Everything was painted white.

We opened in May, and quickly saw a hundred people a week dropping in to use it. It was mainly the workers who came, not holidaymakers, and that's how we wanted it to be. Bar owners and others also started to send people to us if they were in trouble. This was a mixture of workers and holidaymakers and we were happy to help both.

We soon found that people who had come to use the computers, or play pool, would drift to the prayer room – not all but some of them. We created the prayer room in such a way that it allowed for exploration but it also contained lots of prayer stations with simply worded explanations to help people engage in prayer who were not used to praying.

People would often say it was an incredibly peaceful environment. People would come in for something practical, like booking a flight, and it might emerge that they were returning to a difficult situation like a serious illness or crisis in the family. We would help them practically by giving them computer access, but also offer to pray with them. Or they might come in because they needed to find somewhere to stay – again we would help however we practically could and offer to pray as well. They might write a prayer for a family member or just sit quietly in there and reflect. It was almost like being chaplains to the workers. We even started doing regular massage and prayer sessions for strippers and prostitutes in the prayer room.

We were simply continuing what we were doing on the street – developing connectedness with workers, being accessible to people – and we started to see small glimmers of hope. Once a worker was out with a friend, selling ketamine, and suddenly said she had to go. Her friend said, 'You're not going to see your Christian friends again?' 'No, I'm not,' she replied, 'I'm going to see my *friends*'. As far as she was concerned, we had become friends and it wasn't important to give us a label. Moments like these reassured us that we were making genuine friends, not just kidding ourselves that we were.

We had a few ground rules – for example we once had to ban one girl because she was uploading her own porn, and we had to stop one or two people from smoking or drinking alcohol on the premises – but generally people respected the centre, people liked coming: they felt safe there.

One of our volunteers pointed out that we were aiming to care for the physical, emotional and spiritual needs of our community. This became a helpful phrase that we used to remind ourselves of what we were about and to explain our work to others. 24-7 Prayer in Ibiza exists to care for the physical, emotional and spiritual needs of the people we meet.

BUILDING A PERMANENT PRAYER SPACE

- Do it well. Make it look nice. 'Shabby chic' often tends to look more shabby than chic! Get someone who loves making their house look good and stylish and invite them to oversee the creation of your room.

- Invest. If you are serious about the creation of a space that facilitates a connection with the divine, you will need to invest a little bit of money into it.

- Avoid clichés – like a giant wave about to wash over you.

- Make it interactive. You can create a variety of stations that people can interact with. Here are some of the ones we used.

  ○ Thanksgiving
  ○ Family
  ○ Jobs
  ○ Health
  ○ Forgiveness/Confession
  ○ The World
  ○ Bottles
  ○ Candles

- Keep it peaceful. Don't make it too busy. Aim for a safe, quiet place, a place of reflection and interaction and peace.

- Ban lists. Resist the temptation to display all your church's activities and overseas missions partners. Let's not perpetuate shopping list praying by the rooms we create. If you want information to be available, put it in folders on shelves.

- Be sensitive. Be aware of the residents and others around you. Don't be a nuisance.

- Be open. If at all possible please, please make your room available to the general public: don't make it a private, Christian-only thing.

- Make it accessible. Attach your prayer room to a café or a drop-in centre. People who come for a coffee or to use the computers will drift to the prayer room.

- Explain. Give simply worded explanations for things like prayer and repentance. But avoid too much religious language.

- Make a prayer wall. Allow people to post a prayer on a wall, or similar, with the assurance that, if they do, people would pray for them. Pray for them. Work out a system: we marked with a green dot sticker once a request had been prayed for.

- Close. Because we work for 24-7 Prayer doesn't mean you need to make your room available 24-7.

- Care. Put someone in charge and encourage everyone to take the upkeep of the room seriously.

STREET PRAYER

STREET PRAYER

6

One night we met three guys dressed as Superman, Spider-Man and Batman. I went up to them and said, 'Hi guys, my name's Brian. I'm a Christian, this is my mate Fiona and she's a Christian, and we'd like to pray for you.' And they said, 'Alright then'.

So we were standing – you've got to think, the square mile with the most pubs, clubs and bars in all of Europe, it's quite a messy floor, I keep my eyes open – and they'd all knelt down. I didn't ask them to – it's already weird and they just made it weirder by all kneeling down in the street. So we knelt down too. It was great – three superheroes kneeling for prayer in the West End – how surreal is that? Spider-Man even cried. (I always knew he was the weaker superhero.)

On the same evening one of our girls prayed for a guy and when she finished he said, 'You must be a f**king mind reader', her prayer was so spot on for his life.

Another guy asked, 'Can you save me?' We said, 'No', but pointed him in the right direction and prayed with him.

A Scottish lad who we talked to said, 'My best friend is a Christian and she told me God was going to get on my case in Ibiza, and now I have met with you lot!' Needless to say we prayed with him.

One worker came to us in tears, asking for prayer because she had no money for food. We prayed with her and bought her some food.

One of our team was praying for someone – a group of full on Tottenham supporters, big guys. At the end of it one of them said, 'Did you feel that?!' After that when we were out he would always ask for prayer and encouraged others to ask for prayer, saying, 'You've got to try this'.

Another time we stopped to talk with two guys and one was giving us serious chat. We saw him the next day and he apologised, he said I need you to pray for me. So we said fine, but then he changed his mind and asked, 'No, could I pray and you say the "Amen"?'

COME, HOLY PEOPLE

I once heard my friend Ian Nicholson say, 'For years the church has prayed that ancient prayer "Come, Holy Spirit". The Holy Spirit wants to say to us, "Come holy people".

I've found he is right. Whenever I'm in a prayer meeting or a prayer room I pray that prayer, 'Come Holy Spirit'. And as I pray that prayer, as I invite the Holy Spirit to come, the Holy Spirit often replies by saying, 'Come holy people'.

Weird isn't it? We ask the Holy Spirit to come and before you know it he turns it back on us! We become the answer to our prayers, we speak to God, we get close to God and he says, 'Come holy people. I'm going to take you out into a world that needs you. Because you are the carriers of me, and you are the light in the darkness and you are the ones who are called to shine and you are the ones who are blessed to bless others. I want to take you out in to a world that needs you.'

Isn't that good, isn't that exciting? We aren't just meant to be like giant sponges, sitting around soaking up God and getting more and more soaked and soaked and soaked and soaked. Sometimes the sponge has to be squeezed! Squeezed out on the world. Some of what we have been soaking up has to be squeezed out on others so that they can know the goodness and grace and the mercy and the redemption and the love and forgiveness of our Lord and Saviour. We are compelled to get out and express all of this but I believe we can only effectively do this when we do it from a place of prayer.

We were compelled to get out on the streets and pray for people. Every night we'd be out on the street, we'd go up to people and ask if they would like prayer. You'd think they would think that was freaky. But every summer people would say, 'Yes. Please pray with me'.

People want prayer. Even many who wouldn't call themselves Christians. We prayed with thousands of people over the years, and I still find myself amazed and humbled by the number of opportunities we got to chat, listen to and pray with people out on the street.

We lived with expectancy, a sense that God would show up, and when we got back to the rest of the team we'd say, 'You'll never believe but we just prayed for ...' and they would go out and come back and say, 'You'll never believe ...' The whole evening would be this interchange of prayer and mission, breathing in and breathing out. That's how it was, how we lived. Just picking people up and taking them home, just trying to be agents of grace.

MISS WORLD PRAYERS

Here's how it goes when we pray for others on the streets. These are the kinds of things people want to pray for and the way in which we do it.

Number one prayer request is always 'others'. People generally want you to pray for someone else. At first I think they feel it's selfish to ask for prayer themselves, often saying things like, 'I don't deserve your prayers but could you pray for my Granny', or a sick loved one, or a friend who is having a hard time.

People often asked us to pray for dead people. We did pray for them but generally turned the prayer to pray for the bereaved family and friends. Often it was as if they wanted us to get a message to their friend or family member, or they just missed them dearly and wanted us to pray that they will be OK in heaven.

Other people asked for what I call 'Miss World' prayers. They would ask us to pray for world peace, for an end to hunger.

Once we have prayed for these things, we tend to ask, 'Is there anything we can pray for you about?' Mostly we would get prayers about the future, meeting the right partner, making enough money, good employment – that kind of thing.

Often as we talked and listened to people it went to a deeper level. The five areas that people talked to us about a lot were: guilt, regret, fear, pain and failure. I think this tended to happen because we took the time, we prayed before we went out, we asked to be led, allowed the Holy Spirit to prompt and guide us and we didn't rush. People were also on holiday so they tended to be more relaxed and in less of a hurry. This is where you really have to believe God will show up, and he does. We'd get a lot of emotional responses as we prayed for people and it was always beautiful to watch God show up and start to interact with people who maybe hadn't given him a lot of thought before.

We would also pray for people to be healed. You'd be surprised by how many people don't want you to do that, but we were never frightened to ask! We prayed for a number of people who have got better.

Of course there were comedy prayer requests like guys asking for longer willies or some asking if Leicester could win the FA cup. We still pin them on our wall and simply pray for the person but not the request!

We worked hard at not using religious language. I have certain phrases that I really pray for our generation. I pray for God to smile on people, to bless their families, to help them in work, to provide all they need. I often also pray for peace. People need peace. We did of course ask the Holy Spirit to lead our praying, but it does help to have given some forethought to what you are going to say.

If people didn't want us to pray for them there and then on the street, we asked if they would like to fill out a prayer request form for us to take back to our prayer room. We'd get them to write it, but if they didn't want to write it we would, and we'd get them to sign it. That way we felt confident that we'd pray their pray accurately.

BEING SAFE, BUILDING TRUST

The first time we went out, we found people were far more open to prayer – to being prayed for on the street – than we had expected. We had seen the previous teams do it, we had watched a British TV documentary about them getting prayer requests, so we had a good idea that it might work. I had read Carla Harding's story in *Red Moon*

Rising[1] about how she had prayed for a guy on the streets of Ibiza and his knee had been healed, so we figured we would just continue in that vein.

The first time I ever asked someone if I could pray for them, I was almost apologetic. It was two girls and it turned out they were from Norfolk, so we had a bit of a connection. We told them what we did, that we where Christians and believed in prayer, and then I think they said something like, 'That's sweet'. Then I just asked, 'Do you mind if we pray for you?' I was expecting them to say, 'No!' – I had low expectations – but they both said, 'Yes'. And what was beautiful is that they both put their hands together in the praying hands position, I prayed a simple prayer for blessing over them, they were very grateful and we left it at that.

Then there was a guy called Paul who didn't want prayer on the street but was happy to let me write a prayer request down for him. That was how we started to write prayers down. At first we used Post-it notes. We went out with a stack of multi-coloured Post-it notes and wrote down prayer requests. We prayed for over a thousand people and the walls of the prayer room were covered from floor to ceiling with Post-it notes. Later we found that people liked to fill out a more official card. So we got some cards printed with our logo on. Branding became important because people could recognise us.

There are some other practical things we learned about going out on the street.

We realised we needed to be recognised, to be identifiable. In Ibiza people promote themselves very blatantly by what they wear. We got used to sights like our neighbour on his mobile phone in his garden, wearing a vest and jeans and thigh-high PVC 12-inch platform boots for his job promoting a club night!

Early on I experimented with wearing a clerical collar down into San Antonio – I did it partly for a dare. But it didn't feel natural and I was very nervous. I remember driving in with the collar on. I stopped at every zebra crossing, indicated at junctions, I even parked legally for a change. Something about the collar made me feel I should

---

[1] *Red Moon Rising*, Pete Greig (Kingsway 2003).

behave properly. I walked the streets – it wasn't busy, there were no dramatic moments, no great conversations, just a few hellos and a couple of jokes, but that was all. The collar definitely didn't work at that moment – and we could hardly get the whole team wearing them or we definitely would have looked like a group of tourists on a stag or hen do!

Then we got T-shirts. The summer teams had T-shirts before, but with a subtle design and you couldn't really see what was on there. We didn't need symbolism or imagery – we just needed our teams to be easily identified. Our T-shirts had a big, bold, 24-7 Ibiza logo – that was all: no Bible verses or religious language. People saw the 24-7 logo and they immediately recognised it, and soon came to trust it, but if we walked out without the T-shirts, those we didn't know so well wouldn't always recognise us.

Once a bartender asked me for a T-shirt and I gave him one – but later I realised I shouldn't have done that. Not because he was doing anything particularly out of order, but it was important for people to be able to see our logo, our brand, and know what it represented. For us it meant: 'The person wearing this T-shirt can be trusted to help you if you're in a muddle and will be more than happy to pray with you.' It became more important still in later years, when staff at the medical centre or the local police would call us to come and assist with someone who needed help. The same branding on our Vomit Van also helped those people to recognise us quickly – as well as looking just that bit more official to the occasional nervous person who desperately needed help but was sensible enough to question the wisdom of jumping into the vehicle of a stranger.

BRANDED

We went out in twos – sometimes threes. But we learned not to send two guys out together – it never worked. For two guys, it was hard to approach girls without seeming to be on the pull, and it was hard to approach blokes without seeming aggressive or odd. It just didn't work. Two girls could approach girls or guys, and a girl and a guy could as well. But two blokes never worked.

Tracy and I didn't often go out together – one of us had to be up to take the kids to school in the morning. As a team we only went out six nights a week. We felt it was important for our team to have one night when everyone could be together without anyone being on duty.

When each new two-week team arrived, we'd take them out on an orientation tour to start with. First we took them out in their ordinary clothes, not with a branded T-shirt on, so they were like ordinary holidaymakers. We were putting them in other people's shoes. Then we took them out with 24-7 Ibiza T-shirts on, so that they would see the difference, the way people reacted. It made initial contact with strangers relatively easy for the new arrivals, because people knew we were the prayer people. They would just walk up to us and ask for prayer. So it didn't matter that new team members had only just arrived and didn't know anybody. And I think a number of our teams were quite pleasantly surprised by how much easier it was than they had expected it to be.

Each team had someone in charge of the evening, generally a long-term team member. They would split the team in two, divide them into pairs, make sure each pair had phones, receive calls back at the centre, co-ordinate the van, keep everyone praying – and generally bring leadership to the evening.

We also had to learn not to allow our work to revolve around the two-week teams. In the first season it was almost as if we were hosting guests. We had been anxious to give them a good time, make sure they went to a few good clubs, got to see the island and different beaches, and generally had a good experience. But we had to remind ourselves that 24-7 Ibiza wasn't there to facilitate a team having a lovely holiday: that was not what anyone had gone through an application process to do. The teams were coming out to serve the work – the work was not there to serve the team.

Of course we were concerned for their well-being, not wanting to see anyone burnt out or distressed by what they did. And we did want them to love their time in Ibiza. But time after time we saw that, in the act of serving, they got loads out of it – even if they didn't get to go to all the places that they wanted. So occasionally someone might arrive saying, 'I need to get to Cream at Amnesia on Thursday night', and whereas at first we would have tried to make that happen, later we'd be firm and say, 'I'm not sure we can do that'.

The general feeling amongst some full-time mission workers is that short, two-week teams are a great deal of hard work for a limited return – and that the benefit is more to the visitors themselves, to their discipleship and to raising their awareness of the issues. The more cynical might say short-term mission is more like Christian tourism.

We wanted to make sure in our situation that even a short-term team would be a genuine blessing and benefit to the work rather than being a burden. We wanted our teams to contribute. And they did, very much so: at the height of the season we would have seriously struggled to sustain the work without their input, particularly the continued prayer and conversation on the streets, as demands for our practical help increased.

BIBLES AND BLESSING

We were always looking for ways to start a prayer conversation. People would often stop us and ask us for a light – so I always had a lighter in my pocket. Eventually we got lighters printed with 'Jesus Light of the World', our logo and our phone number. It was cheesy – but it would often start a conversation.

We found generosity worked: people responded to us giving things away for free. We wanted to welcome people, to bless them. In the early days, teams gave out oranges and other fruit during the night, but we had to stop that because the police were concerned we'd injected something into them. But we were able to give out oranges during the day on the beach, and to ask people if they wanted prayer.

One day Michael was on the beach, giving out oranges, and was called over by three topless girls. It turned out one of them was a very attractive, award-winning beauty queen. They asked him to explain his faith. He told them what Christ meant to him and did a really great job of conveying the gospel to them – but he later said, 'Never, in all my life, have I maintained such good eye contact while sharing the gospel.'

But we wanted to give people a Bible. We had found these *Jesus Loves Porn Stars* Bibles – by XXX Church – a great organisation working with strippers and the porn industry in America. We bought four hundred of these from America, for £2.50 each. They were bright pink and yellow and had the image of a stereotypical seventies male porn star on the front (just his head!). The cover caught people's interest and they were surprised to find that it was a Bible. And even more surprised to find that, in *The Message* translation, they could understand a Bible when they began to read it. We started giving them out, and people loved them. Some even saw a friend's copy and came to seek us out to get their own.

We got some great responses. I gave one to a bouncer friend, and later he came out of the club and said, 'I've read that Brian – I've changed a few bits, made a few corrections. ...' Then one bloke was going into the club with his mates, he looked at the bouncer with a smile on his face and said, 'I'm going to need prayer for this'. So the bouncer, an ex-soldier, got the Bible out and read him a Psalm! Another one thought Matthew was a really rubbish start for a book – Mark would be better because no-one starts a book with a genealogy.

One time a girl ran up to us saying, 'Revelation – effin' heavy – when I got to that bit ...' Another girl said, 'Someone stole my Bible, I need another one'. And one time, three guys standing outside a strip club called us over to say they were taking the Bibles with them on holiday. They said unbelievably good things about the Bibles.

One guy had the gospel summed up quite accurately. He'd gone home, read the entire book of Matthew and came back observing that, 'All those people kept wanting Jesus to give them a sign that he was God, but he wouldn't do it – it was like he just kept saying: I just want you to trust me'.

We had to trust the Bible to do the Bible's work, to allow the narrative to speak for itself. Seeing the Bible at work outside a Christian context, in a totally alien environment, was interesting and powerful. People didn't want notes explaining it to them – they just wanted to engage with it.

Four hundred Bibles went in four months – all to people who weren't Christians – and we realised God was getting his Word out on the street. Eventually we got our own really attractive *Jesus Loves Ibiza* Bibles printed.

This what we wrote on the back of them:

Does Jesus Really Love Ibiza?

Totally. We don't know what you think about Jesus, but we do know that he loves this beautiful island and all who inhabit it. Jesus loves everyone, regardless of race, gender or social standing. Following Jesus is a bit like dancing. The wrong things that we have done have put us out of step with God and left us in a mess that we can't get out of by ourselves, but Jesus made a way to rescue us if we follow Him.

Following Him is about catching his rhythm and allowing your life to be moved to the rhythm of his beat! His dance is a dance of love, mercy, justice, forgiveness, selflessness and sacrifice. It's a dance that leads us to repentance and relationship with God.

So what you have here is part of the Bible that tells the story of Jesus; it communicates his rhythm. The author Eugene Peterson wanted to get the Bible back to its roots, to the way we talk when we are not trying to sound religious. Whether you have been reading the Bible for years or you're exploring it for the first time, *The Message* will surprise you. In it you will read about the love revolution that inspired the women and men who first experienced it to dance to a different rhythm and change the world forever.

'Come to me. Get away with me and you'll recover your life. I'll show you how to take a real rest. Walk with me and work with me – watch how I do it. Learn the unforced rhythms of grace. I won't lay anything heavy or ill-fitting on you. Keep company with me and you'll learn to live freely and lightly.'

Jesus

We found it worked: it opened up conversations, and it gave us opportunities to pray even more with people. We all made a conscious effort never to give a Bible away without writing something meaningful in the front to the recipient. I had one guy come up to me a year or so after being given a Bible saying that the verse I had written in the front about not worrying had stuck with him all year.

We even had a report from one of our team members who attended a baptism in England: when the guy got up to share his testimony, one of the reasons he started searching was because on holiday in Ibiza someone had given him a Bible!

> A friend of mine was up country this week and went to a baptism with fifteen people. One of the guys shared his testimony. ... He was out in Ibiza last summer and met one of the 24-7 Ibiza teams who gave him a Bible and told him about Jesus. When he got back to the UK, another guy asked him whether he wanted to go through the Bible together, which he was apparently stunned by, but because of his encounter with 24-7 he decided he would! Now he's given his life to Jesus and been baptised!! Praise God He IS following people.

This all came from a commitment to pray with people on the streets. Over the years while we were in Ibiza, we noticed that this was definitely on God's agenda. At the same time there was a 'Healing on the Streets' initiative born in the UK and the wonderful phenomena of 'treasure hunting' and all that was happening in Redding, California. God very definitely has been and is continuing to propel his people out to find new and innovative ways of connecting with people and to pray on the streets.

If reading this chapter has inspired you to get out there on the street, then I will list a few helpful tips which I think would stand you in good stead as you to get out there and truly connect wherever you are. Personally I think you will find God very active and at work on the streets. I am often struck by Ezekiel's prophetic image – the further away the river flowed from the temple, the deeper it became (Ezekiel 47). I think we could liken that a little to prayer on the streets: the further we physically move away from what we know to be the normal place for prayer and encounter, the deeper it will become.

POINTERS FOR PRAYING ON THE STREET

- Take the time to pray before you go out – ask to be lead, allow the Holy Spirit to prompt and guide you – don't rush. Give some thought to what you might pray.

- Try to pray for the person themselves. People generally want you to pray for someone else. Pray for them – but then ask again, 'Is there anything we can pray for you about?'

- If people ask for prayer for dead people, pray – but turn the prayer to pray for the bereaved family and friends.

- Talk and listen to people, and it may go to a deeper level. The five areas that people talked to us a lot about were: guilt, regret, fear, pain and failure.

- Pray for people to be healed.

- Don't use religious language.

- If people don't want prayer there and then, ask if you can pray for them when they have gone. If you have a prayer room, write down and pin up their prayer request in there.

- Be light hearted about comedy prayer requests: if you can turn it to something more serious that's great – but don't be too upset if someone isn't taking it seriously.

- Join in the fun. If you see a hen party, you could ask to pray for the bride – if it's a stag do, ask which is the lucky man!

Come Holy Spirit,
fill the hearts of your faithful,
kindle in them the fire of your love.
Send forth your Spirit and they shall be created.
And You shall renew the face of the earth.
Through Christ Our Lord, Amen.

Catholic prayer

HAVE YOU COME TO SAVE MY SOUL?

7

One night Tracy and Rachel were out on the West End. This is what Tracy wrote:

Rachel and I are part way through our allotted hour out and about on the streets in the West End of San Antonio. As we casually chat to a friendly PR at Godfather's bar, out of the corner of my eye, I notice a guy stumble as he leaves the bar, half-sitting, half-falling into a chair on the outside terrace. He puts his head in his hands for a few moments, but then lifts his head and seems to be OK, so we carry on chatting.

It's not a deep conversation – just catching up with a worker that we regularly see and he's working so we don't want to keep him chatting for too long. We finish our chat and turn to leave – I glance towards the stumbling guy, just to check that he's still OK. I'm not staring at him, but as I look over, his eyes meet mine – he stands up and walks towards us, more steadily than I expect.

'Have you come to save my soul?'

'What did you say?' I ask, a little taken aback by his opening line.

'Have you come to save my soul?' he repeats, more insistently this time.

'Well …' I begin.

'You're like my friend, Robert', he interrupts, 'I can see it in you. You're the same'. He's being quite serious.

'What do you mean?' I ask, intrigued.

'You're a Christian aren't you? I know you are. I can tell'.

I find this a very strange story, primarily because Tracy doesn't look like a man called Robert! Then, on another night, this happened to Tracy:

Becky and I have ventured into Tropicana. The club is packed and we are looking out for someone that might be in there, but it's crowded and we haven't spotted them yet. Someone falls heavily onto my shoulder and continues to hang on to me: I turn to see a young, blonde girl clutching my shoulder. She's dressed for a night out and I imagine she looked lovely at the start of the evening; now her face is streaked with mascara and her eyes are wide and frightened.

'Help me!' she gasps.

'Are you OK?' I ask – a stupid question really, given what she's just said and the way she's clinging to me.

'Please help me,' she says, still holding on tightly, 'I'm scared. I don't know who to trust.'

I take her arm, tell her to come with me, and steer her through the crowd and out of the door, away from the noise and madness of the club. I help her to sit down on one of the white plastic chairs on the club's outdoor terrace; she grips my hand as I ask her what's wrong.

I'm not an expert, but it quickly becomes clear to me that she's taken Ecstasy: like many under the effects of Ecstasy, she's gurning – grinding her teeth. The sound is horrible – like she is crunching a mouthful of boiled sweets – and I'm convinced she must be breaking her teeth, but she can't control her jaw so she carries on. I give her some chewing gum, hoping to spare her teeth, her tongue and the inside of her cheeks.

She tells me that she's never taken any sort of drug before – she doesn't ever do this back home. She took half of an Ecstasy pill tonight for the first time. She doesn't make excuses for that: she took the half voluntarily – she wanted to see what it was like, wanted to have good holiday – and anyway, all her friends were doing it. Later in the evening, her friend had popped another whole one into her mouth and she tells me that she swallowed it without really thinking about what she was doing. Now she's frightened.

'What's that noise?' she asks me, and I tell her she's grinding her teeth. 'Why am I doing that? Why can't I stop it?' so I explain that it's just one of the effects of the pills she's taken.

'Am I going to die?' she panics again, 'I don't want to die'.

She's not in the worst state I've seen and I'm pretty sure she just needs some time for the drug to pass through her system.

'Don't leave me, please don't leave me,' she begs, 'I'm scared.'

I promise to stay with her until she feels safe; I tell her that I'll keep watching over her and that if she gets worse, I'll call an ambulance or get her to the medical centre straight away.

Her friend has found us now – she's also taken pills and has been drinking heavily. Moods begin to swing around all over the place. At first it's all very tearful and emotional; Sarah, the newly arrived friend, is promising to look after Emily, the girl that bumped into me in the club. She's keen to demonstrate her competence, she knows exactly what to do, she's seen it all before.

Sarah tells Emily that she's been so worried about her, she loves her so much. But Emily is upset with Sarah for giving her the extra pill and won't go with her – she says she wants to stay with me. Now Sarah is angry with me – why am I interfering when it's none of my f***ing business? It all starts to get a bit heated.

Eventually things calm down. Brian comes with the vomit van and we take both girls (plus another that Becky has been looking after while I've been with Emily) back to their hotel. I stay with Emily in her hotel room until she feels like she's back to normal. When we leave several hours later the sun is up, but it's been a good night's work. I'm glad I was there.

What intrigues me about both situations is that Emily and the guy at Godfather's saw something ...

How did Robert's friend know Tracy was a Christian before she had even spoken to him? She was wearing a 24-7 Ibiza T-shirt, but he'd never heard of us – so it wasn't that. What did he see that made him get up from his table to ask a complete stranger if she had come to save his soul?

And why did the girl Emily cling onto Tracy like that and beg her – someone she had never met in her life – not to leave her when she was already scared and feeling that she didn't know who to trust?

Tracy is by no means the only one this sort of thing has ever happened to – many of our team members have similar stories to tell.

On another night Tracy and Rachel are once more out together when this happened:

> We spot a big group of girls, all dressed in short red skirts and devil horns – it's a hen night. We look at each other, raise our eyebrows simultaneously, each answering the other's unspoken question – 'Shall we?' 'Come on then', says Rachel, and we approach the group and introduce ourselves. We ask if we can say a prayer for the bride-to-be.
>
> Our prayers are well received and we start to make a move, thinking that the moment is over – but a couple of the girls call us back to ask some questions about what we believe. One of the girls starts to confide in Rachel, telling her some of her story; Rachel listens and then gently prays for her and she begins to cry. One of the other girls sees the tears and springs to her friend's defence.
>
> 'What did she say to you?' she demands 'Why is she making you cry?'
>
> Rachel feels awkward, but before she can explain, the girl she's just prayed for answers her friend, 'It's not her that's making me cry,' she says, 'It's God in her that's touching me.'

The reason these kinds of things happened and keep happening is to do with a life of prayer and connectedness. You see, before we went out every evening, we prayed – I mean we really prayed. In fact our summers were immersed in prayer.

We weren't just sitting shouting at God: it was all manner of prayer – it was reflective, it was peaceful, it was intercessory, it was meditative. We had moments of intense honesty admitting defeat, frustration and guilt. We also had moments of incredible childlikeness where we left feeling our God could do anything.

It was a prayerful existence. Our summers in Ibiza involved some of the most focussed and intense times of prayer I have ever experienced. They were also some of the most boring, long and hard times of prayer I have ever experienced. But we definitely prayed.

So, when we go out, perhaps it's this that happens:

> By their fruit you will recognise them. Do people pick grapes from thorn-bushes, or figs from thistles? Likewise, every good tree bears good fruit, but a bad tree bears bad fruit. A good tree cannot bear bad fruit, and a bad tree cannot bear good fruit. Every tree that does not bear good fruit is cut down and thrown into the fire. Thus, by their fruit you will recognise them.
>
> Matthew 7:16–20

People recognise us by our fruit! They see something hanging on us that is different! The Greek word for fruit here is *karpos*.

As you follow that word throughout the Bible you find it in Galatians: 'But the fruit of the Spirit is love, joy, peace, forbearance, kindness, goodness, faithfulness, gentleness and self-control. Against such things there is no law' (Galatians 5:22–23).

This is the fruit I think people see: they see all of this hanging on our lives and they are drawn to it, they recognise it as different and us as different!

People see something in us – a reflection, perhaps. We carry something. We carry the fruit of the Spirit and people recognise something that is different. That fruit grows in us as we meditate on the Word. In the Greek version of the Old Testament, that same word *karpos* is used:

> Blessed is the one
>   who does not walk in step with the wicked
> or stand in the way that sinners take
>   or sit in the company of mockers,
> but whose delight is in the law of the Lord,
>   and who meditates on his law day and night.
> That person is like a tree planted by streams of water,
>   which yields its fruit in season
> and whose leaf does not wither –
>   whatever they do prospers.
>
> Psalm 1:1–3

The fruit grows when we meditate on the God's word, day and night. Meditating on the word is a form of prayer, focusing on Christ, becoming prayerful people.

That word 'meditate' is closely linked to the word 'ruminate' – which means to ponder thoughtfully but can also be linked to a sense of chewing something over. God's word gets chewed over, we absorb it into ourselves, it has an effect and grows fruit in us. 'Ruminate' is linked to the Latin word which means to chew the cud. This is in reference to many domesticated animals, especially cows, who chew and chew their food, then regurgitate it and chew it some more – they thoroughly digest everything they eat. By this process of constant chewing and regurgitating, they get maximum nourishment from all they eat.

That's meditation – that's what prayer and reflection and immersing ourselves in God's word will bring: maximum nutrition from our maker, which I believe in turns causes fruit to grow on our lives. I've heard people say, 'Preach the gospel, and if necessary, use words', and I do understand what they are trying to communicate, but if that lack of words is not backed up by a meditative lifestyle, no one will notice a thing.

Then we start to yield fruit in season. The fruit of our meditation and reflection on God's word and prayerful lives should be the fruit of the Spirit. Then as we walk about through life, people notice something that is different – and they reach out to grab you or approach you with questions about their destiny, or feel a touch from God himself.

As we pray and live a prayerful life and abide in him, then we see fruit.

> I am the true vine, and my Father is the gardener. He cuts off every branch in me that bears no fruit, while every branch that does bear fruit he prunes so that it will be even more fruitful. You are already clean because of the word I have spoken to you. Remain in me, as I also remain in you. No branch can bear fruit by itself; it must remain in the vine. Neither can you bear fruit unless you remain in me.
>
> I am the vine; you are the branches. If you remain in me and I in you, you will bear much fruit; apart from me you can do nothing. If you do not remain in me, you are like a branch that is thrown away and withers; such branches are picked up, thrown into the fire and burned. If you remain in me and my words remain in you, ask whatever you wish, and it will be done for you. This is to my Father's glory, that you bear much fruit, showing yourselves to be my disciples.
>
> John 15:1–8

Tracy's stories are not about her looking like an awesome Christian or performing some form of pre-planned outreach strategy. They are about abiding in Christ.

Prayer and mission is about the close interconnectedness we have to the vine. If I want to be fruitful, to have a life that produces fruit, then it won't come about solely by going to loads of different meetings and reading loads of books. It won't come about by me screwing up my face and striving to be fruitful. It won't even come about by me going out determined to pray with as many people on the streets of San Antonio as I can. In fact I sometimes think there is a false pressure on us around the misunderstanding of what it means to be fruitful.

We would often pick people up from the airport to come and serve on summer teams and as they jumped into the car, one of the first things some would say is, 'How many people have you seen saved?' This can sometimes be translated 'How fruitful is what you are doing?' I am all about people getting saved – I give my life for it. But this question comes loaded with so much pressure, it seems to be about numbers, and makes us try to deliver numbers!

But the secret of fruitfulness is this: 'Remain in me, as I also remain in you.'

Fruitfulness is not achieved by striving for numerical success. Fruitfulness comes from simply being connected to Jesus. I have a mental image of a branch lying on its own trying to produce fruit, straining really hard to make something happen – to pop out an orange or something like that. But you know that, because it is not connected to the tree, it will fail! Nothing will happen – there will be no fruit. Jesus says: 'apart from me you can do nothing'. The branch needs to be connected to the vine. We do this in prayer and meditation and if we continue to abide in him, receiving lots of nurturing sap and life-giving nutrients, the fruit will come.

We told loads of stories about what happened out on the streets, because they were interesting and made for good blogging and preaching – but we learnt that the biggest story was that we prayed. We abided in him and then, as we walked about, people recognised us as fruit-bearing individuals.

We abide by absorbing, praying, listening, singing, reading, memorising, learning – and then continuing to act out of what we have absorbed and read and learned and taken in when we are out on the streets of Ibiza, or doing our jobs, or collecting the kids from school. Abiding is staying with the Lord, walking with him, accepting his rule. All this is prayerful abiding. If people recognise us as *loving, joyful, peaceful, patient, kind, good, faithful, gentle and self-controlled*, I am pretty sure they will be drawn to us.

There is an ancient form of meditation called *lectio divina*. Here is a pattern that I have loosely based on that. For me it does help to think about my posture, my breathing, and to avoid any possible distraction. The only physical comfort I think about is whether I am sitting comfortably and in a place that is conducive to reflection.

- Sit straight and comfortably.
- Get your breathing right, ensure it is balanced, even and steady.
- Spend time sitting quietly.

- Write down any distractions, put them to one side and pick them up later.

- Choose a Bible verse, maybe read it through seven to ten times.

- Allow that one verse to roll around in your mind.

- At other times memorise scripture – maybe specific scriptures for specific situations.

- Pray repetitive prayers – it's okay.

- Write prayers out, repeat them.

- Focus on the names and characteristics of Jesus, mull them over.

THE VOMIT VAN

THE VOMIT VAN

Becoming the answer to our own prayers ...

One night in July 2006, Tracy was late getting back. As it got later and later, and she still wasn't back, I began to get restless and annoyed. I wasn't worried, just a little frustrated that we had a busy day ahead and she was going to be getting only about three hours sleep. I didn't phone as I knew if there was anything really difficult, she would phone me. I occasionally worry but this is something I have to deal with and try not to transmit to Tracy. We have always felt incredibly safe operating within the West End and its surrounds.

Eventually at 5.30, Tracy stumbled in, very tired. She began to explain ...

After they had sent the two-week team of young volunteers back to the hotel, at 2.30 am, Tracy and two long-termers, Indya and Johanna, set off on the three-mile drive back home to their own beds.

Driving through the narrow streets of San Antonio, they saw a guy lying face down in the middle of the road in front of them, and had to stop the car. They phoned the emergency services and police and paramedics came quickly, and took the guy off to the medical centre in an ambulance.

Continuing their journey, they were about half-way home when they spotted a group of people on the street outside a club – some vomiting, some sprawled out on the pavement, a couple of girls a bit unsteady on their feet, trying without success to wave down a taxi. Wondering what on earth was going on, Tracy and the girls stopped the car for the second time.

They approached the group, but a couple of holiday reps, who worked for a company that catered for 18- to 30-year-old holidaymakers, assured them that they were experienced with this sort of thing and that Tracy and the girls should just go home and leave them to it. Not being entirely convinced, the three of them stood at a slight distance, watching to see what would develop. Before long, the holiday reps grew weary of the situation and abandoned the group of holidaymakers, so Tracy, Indya and Johanna returned.

There was still no luck with the taxis – you couldn't blame them really for not wanting to take someone who might very well throw up. If someone vomits in your cab, it's your night's business ruined!

Gradually some of the group sobered up enough either to walk or to get a taxi, but one lad remained, lying on the pavement. The girls caught the attention of someone working at the club and asked for some water, thinking maybe a drink would help. The guy nodded, went inside the club and returned with a large glass of water, and then threw it in the face of the drunk guy – not quite what the girls had in mind!

Trying again to get some water for him to drink, they were told, 'No!' – because the bar was now closed for the night. So they sat with him for a while until he began to sober up a little.

Another guy, sitting up, swaying a bit, ponderously looked down at himself and noticed the mess he was in – dirty, wet, covered in his own vomit. Disgusted, he ripped the dirtiest sleeve off his Hugo Boss shirt, got up and staggered off, determined he could now get back to his hotel on his own. Finally, left with just two girls, they decided the best thing would be to put them in our car and take them to where they needed to be – before finally making their way home.

GRACE

I confess I was not particularly gracious when I heard why Tracy was so late home. I had one of those, 'It's hardly like they are unfortunate orphans who deserve our mercy – they bring it on themselves', moments!

Why couldn't Tracy have driven another way home? Why should we do this? It's thankless and frustrating. Why do some people keep serving the customers then refuse them water? Why do the holiday reps take these guys out and get them hammered? It's about money and it annoys me.

All these thoughts raged through my mind.

Then the Lord pushed the word 'grace' into my mind. I need to be constantly reminded of grace. It's not a lesson we learn once: it's something we keep getting dragged back to. I'm not sure we always appreciate it, but it's the echo of this gospel of grace that resonates deep in our souls. Grace in all things – this is our mission.

And I remembered. How many times has God picked me up when *I* have failed? How many times has God stopped for *me*, and not driven past? How many times has God wiped the puke of my sin from *my* face? How many times has God waited patiently by my side until *I* woke up and came to my senses? How many times have I staggered off on my journey without realising that, whilst I was asleep, God had been sitting watching over *me*?

Countless times.

So I returned to that place of grace again. It's not the only time that I've lost grace, and sadly it probably won't be the last, but I'm learning that the trick is to keep coming back to it in prayer as quickly as possible. Ibiza has tested my grace but I hope it has also made me grow in grace.

2 Peter 3:18 says: 'But grow in the grace and knowledge of our Lord and Saviour Jesus Christ.'

This whole incident turned out to be one of those little *ahem* moments, when God interrupted our routine and moved the work up to another level.

Because up to that point, for our first few months in Ibiza, we had spent our time just talking and praying with people. We might have occasionally helped a drunk person but that was all – it wasn't a massive part of what we did. The evening's work would start at around eleven and we usually headed back home between two and three in the morning.

But after all this, and after the Lord had touched my heart about my attitude, we decided as a team that we'd intentionally keep our eyes open for people in a muddle – and we'd go and get our cars and pick them up and take them to safety.

Be careful how you pray. We had prayed, we had seen the mess, and the Lord touched our hearts. We then became the answer to our own prayer. James says this:

> Suppose a brother or a sister is without clothes and daily food. If one of you says to them, "Go in peace; keep warm and well fed," but does nothing about their physical needs, what good is it? In the same way, faith by itself, if it is not accompanied by action, is dead.

> James 2:15–17

Faith needs action, and that's how we wanted to be. But I'm not sure we really knew what that would mean.

WHAT HAVE YOU GOT IN YOUR HAND?

Once again we were drawn to that line in Exodus 4:2, where God says to Moses 'What have you got in your hand?' It was just as if he was repeating himself! We had our cars. So we used them to pick people up and take them back to their hotels.

Sometimes we can be guilty of waiting until all the right things are in place before we do something. We just tried to get on with it, with what we had in our hands.

There shouldn't be a long gap between prayer and mission. If you are praying to own a house one day that people can come to for safety, please start using your sofa as a place people can crash for the night. If you want to have big community meals in a big farmhouse, start having people round to your flat and get them eating food off a tray! Use what you have in your hand.

The Lord responds to this kind of living.

But it was challenging. One of our team, Fiona, only had a two-door Peugeot – it would be impossible to manoeuvre a drunk into the back, so one of us would end up propping them up in the front and then sitting in the back with our arms around them so they didn't slump onto her whilst she was driving.

Our own family car was used a lot. One night we found two girls asleep outside. People were laughing at them, taking photos and generally mocking them. Then to our surprise their father came over. He had taken his 14- and 17-year-old daughters out for a drink but someone, he thought, had spiked their drinks. It was mayhem – there were so many people trying to get involved. We took charge and dragged them out of the West End to the taxi rank, with more puking along the way. The taxi drivers wouldn't take them, so I left them with Rachel and some other members of the team and went to get my car.

Meanwhile the father went to find some water. (We had already given them some but he was drunk too.) On my way back I saw him running up the road, so I jumped out of the car and ran through the crowds after him. I found him bruised and covered in blood. He had confronted some people he thought had sold his girls drugs and they had beaten him up. He was lucky he hadn't been stabbed.

I turned him around and started to walk him out of the West End towards the car to take him back to his daughters, when we were confronted by the seven very angry-looking guys who had just beaten him up. I thought we are going to get the poo kicked out of us. So I put my hand up and said, 'It's okay, I'm taking him home'. The lead guy winked and nodded at me and they let us both pass.

When we finally got the guy and his two daughters to the car, the youngest wet herself on the back seat.

By the time we got them back to their hotel, one of the girl's bags had gone missing, but there was nothing we could do about that. We got them sorted and I talked to the dad. He cried – and I felt tremendous pain for this man. When we went back to the prayer room, I didn't know how to pray, so I just recited the Lord's Prayer – and cried too.

When I did eventually get home, I had to get the car ready for the school run which Tracy was about to do in three hours' time. I tried to clear up some of the dad's excess blood that had got smeared on there, put a towel on the seat of the car because it was still damp from the girl's urine, and left Tracy a note saying, '"Please get the boys to sit on the left side of the back seat as a girl wet herself in the car last night!"'

I wrote about this incident on my blog – and mentioned that we thought maybe it was time to get a van that all of the longer term team would be able to drive and use, specifically for helping people out. It needed to be easy to get in and out of and have the space to manoeuvre drunk people, buckets and team members around inside. Air-conditioning would be really useful. It didn't need to be new – just reliable and a good work horse: after all this was going to be a utility vehicle that would see its fair share of mess.

Within one week we had been given all the money we needed to buy what would quickly become affectionately known as the Vomit Van.

For us, someone else became the answer to our prayers by donating money for the first van. When it broke down, someone else stepped up to the mark and donated money so that we could keep going. It's funny but in many ways they became the answer to the prayer. I love that the church is so wide and that someone, sitting at home in another country, can become the answer to the prayer – and by doing so, they buy us a van that enables lives to be saved on the streets.

LET YOUR GOOD DEEDS SHINE BEFORE MEN

The van was a heart response to a need that God drew to our attention. But there was a benefit that came as the working community witnessed our actions.

We had our logo painted on the side of the van, so that people knew they weren't being kidnapped by some randomers!

From that point on, to the workers, we were no longer just the people who prayed – now we were also the people who helped; I mean we had always helped but it just seemed to go to a different level. Matthew 5:16 says, '... let your light shine before others, that they may see your good deeds and glorify your Father in heaven'.

Our reputation changed dramatically when we started helping people practically as well as praying for them. People started to notice us more, they phoned us more, they chatted more. Female workers would say, at the end of their shift, 'Could you guys walk me home please?' So we would. We went from being the prayer people – the slightly weird Christians who prayed – to being the people to come to for help, the people who were willing to get dirty, the people who could be trusted.

It still took a few years before we had consistent trust from those in authority – from the health centre, from hotel owners, from the police. But there was a clear change when we started to help.

Over the next years, our Vomit Van went from strength to strength. Each season we used it to deal with hundreds of incidents. Most lasted between thirty minutes and two hours! But they all resulted in vulnerable people being helped and taken to a place of safety.

We helped many different people in many different states to get home.

We took people to the health centre for minor injuries; we took them back to their villas, their hotels, and their hostels. We took wealthy people and poor people. We took students, teachers, footballers, bar workers, merchant bankers, prostitutes, mechanics, builders. We took teenagers and forty-somethings. We took children with drunk parents, parents with drunk children.

We took the people who occupy the middle ground: too much of a mess for a taxi, not in enough of a mess for an ambulance. People who were drunk, drugged, lost, disorientated, vulnerable, injured or distressed. Sometimes alone, sometimes struggling to get home with friends. We found some as we walked; we were called to others by workers or bar owners that had spotted them. The local health centre phone us for help: to take someone home who has received treatment, to take someone to the main hospital on the other side of the island for an X-ray, or just to help with communication problems.

The van seats have seen just about every type of bodily fluid – vomit, blood, urine, fæces, sweat, snot and tears – not everything makes it into the bucket! And after each messy night, our team painstakingly cleans up before they stumble into their beds, so that this doesn't all get baked in as the sun gets up a few short hours later.

We gradually became better equipped at being the prayer – bottled water, sick buckets, bin liners, tissues, wet wipes, gloves, plasters. We even got a wheelchair to spare our backs when we were carrying people from the pedestrianised West End to a place where the van could stop.

Apart from the drunkenness, the van has seen all sorts of scenes: broken bones, tear-gassed faces, crushed Ecstasy pills, Rolexes. Prayers and confessions too – an aggressive man maintaining a disturbing monologue of how he'd like to rape and strangle women, a guy so convinced that we were going to rape and knife *him* that he asked us to do it quickly from behind so he wouldn't see it coming, a girl using the seat arms to masturbate. And mixed in with it, every kind of emotion: laughter, weeping, embarrassment, shame, fear, love, hatred, relief, gratitude. Who would have imagined what could come about through such a simple tool?

We were just responding, just trying to help, just being the prayer.

Don't pray if you don't expect it to change your life. Don't *pray* for your community, if you are not willing to be led out of your comfort zone *into* your community. It can sound harsh but I am convinced that if you take your prayer life seriously, you cannot help but become the prayer.

When it comes to getting out on the street and impacting your community here are some helpful pointers:

- Be aware of who is already there. We never wanted to steal taxi drivers' business – there may be other agencies doing what you want to do: find them and join in with them.

- Always operate with a minimum of two people when walking the streets.

- If in doubt about someone who has had too much to drink, or you suspect may have taken too many drugs, always phone an ambulance.

- First aid training is really helpful for anyone who works in busy bar areas.

- Have something – a card or written description – that you can give to people to let them know who you are and how they can contact you later.

- Get practical before you get spiritual! Being practical *is* being spiritual!

- Have a bag. Check out what people need in your situation. One group we know give out free flip flops to people who lose their shoes or are so drunk they can't walk in heels! We always carried water, plasters, tissues, wet wipes, and rubber gloves!

- Be patient. Be a bringer of peace and don't add to the drama.

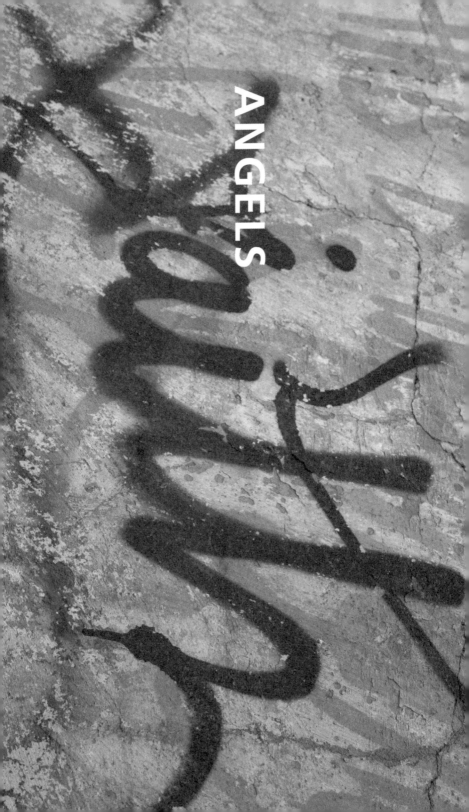

ANGELS

ANGELS 9

About thirty people were packed into our centre on a hot and humid Sunday in September, some on chairs, others sitting on the floor or standing at the back. We'd just sung a couple of songs, which had become the pattern for our Sunday evening gatherings, and now three girls – Claire, Poppy and Angel – were going to sing a song for us that they had been preparing that week.

The first verse of the song was a solo for Angel; as Claire gently strummed the guitar, Angel closed her eyes, lifted her face towards heaven and sang these lines:

> Wonderful, so wonderful,
>   is your unfailing love –
>   your cross has spoken mercy over me.
> No eye has seen, no ear has heard,
>   no heart could fully know –
>   how glorious, how beautiful you are![1]

Twenty-seven-year-old Angel had become our friend over the course of the summer. She loved to sing and worship God and, as she had shared her story with us, it was really evident that she loved God.

Angel's friends smiled with pride as they listened, while most of our team struggled to fight back tears. I must admit I was bit of a mess – I was so moved to hear this beautiful woman sing of the love and mercy of God, knowing that even that night, she would be back out on the streets of the West End, working as a prostitute.

We first began to notice the African girls who work in San Antonio as prostitutes during the summer of 2006. Mostly they seemed to stand around on the streets a short distance from the bright lights of the West End itself, looking for customers leaving the

---

[1] *Beautiful One* Tim Hughes (2004).

bars and clubs and heading back to their hotels and apartments. As the night stretched on, they gradually moved in closer to where there were more people. The nature of their trade was common knowledge, but I was still taken aback one night to see a girl spit out a mouthful of semen right outside our centre, just as her customer went on his way.

We didn't actually get to talk to any of these girls that first year, but we did begin to include the girls in our prayers as we prayed for all the people living, working and holidaying in San Antonio.

The girls disappeared from the largely deserted streets over the winter. That winter we really prayed for them. One of our team, Helen, was particularly inspired to pray, and she kept them at the forefront of our prayer agenda. Tears were cried and we really started to call out to God that somehow he would give us a connection with these girls. We prayed and prayed. It was all we could do.

The next season, summer 2007, the girls returned with the next influx of tourists. We tried to make a connection with the girls who we saw, but we had no clue how to begin. We were unsure who might be controlling them or how they would feel about us trying to talk with them. Would we get ourselves into trouble? Would we get the girls into trouble? We couldn't do much more than smile and say, 'Hello'. If we were feeling particularly brave, we might manage the occasional, 'God loves you', trying to convey with our eyes the sincerity of our words. But the girls seemed wary, unsure how to – or whether to – respond to our friendly greetings, and always watchful for the police or for whoever was keeping an eye on them. We didn't get a lot back from them.

It was especially awkward for our male team members. How do you know what to say or do? We debated paying a girl for some of her time and taking her for something to eat or drink rather than asking her to carry out her usual work. We wondered whether any of them would accept a direct offer of prayer, as so many other unexpected people had done. We eventually decided not to pay for their time but just kept praying for the girls themselves – and for wisdom and inspiration.

We realised that we would have to be persistent and patient in these prayers. With no significant breakthrough, and a continuing sense of helplessness, we carried on praying. We didn't have one significant conversation. We didn't get any direct response from any of the girls. Not one.

More than a year of prayer and nothing! These girls were like ice to us. So we did what any self-respecting prayer organisation would do. We kept praying. We kept praying, kept smiling at them, kept asking God for a breakthrough, kept weeping in the prayer room. It was all we could do. We just had to persevere.

It was not until the summer season of 2008 that we had those first few breakthrough moments. One night, Tash and Nicky spotted someone lying flat on his back on the beach. Like all of our team members, they were alert to noticing people in need of help, so naturally went over to check on him. It transpired that this Swedish American lad was fine – in fact he was pondering the stars and the beauty of the night sky. Tash and Nicky sat down with him.

As they did, two African girls came literally running over, pushed themselves into the middle of the trio on the beach and asked for chewing gum. Tash happily handed them some gum, and they began to talk. Sarah and Julia had been running because they had spotted the police. The easiest place for them to hide was amongst other people, in the hope that they could pass as part of a group of tourists enjoying a night out. These were intelligent girls, fluent in several languages, yet working as prostitutes far from home.

As Tash and Nicky shared the story back in the prayer room, they learned that the group who had been praying while they were out on the streets had once more been praying for the African ladies. The prayer had been that they would not view our team with suspicion and apprehension but would come to us – and to God – as a place of refuge! We sensed God was on the move. At last we saw a chink, a glimpse of God pushing back the darkness. Inspired by that twenty-minute connection, we pushed on, persevered, kept going, kept praying. After two years of prayer, we felt our spirits lift.

One evening, just a few weeks later, Chris and Amanda set out, a bit tired and weary, but in their willingness to serve, praying that God would lead them to the dark places and let their light shine. At first they walked past a small group of African ladies with nothing more than the usual, 'Hello'. Then Chris felt God say to him, incredibly clearly, 'Chris, stop being a wimp, stop walking around and over the things I have put in your path'.

They walked back and sat down on the bench near where the girls were standing. Tired, nervous, wondering what Jesus would do, Chris sent up *'Help me!'* prayers to God and then blurted out, 'Excuse me ... can I talk to you guys for a while?'

And, that simply, God opened a door.

The girls gathered around with smiles as Chris and Amanda introduced themselves and 24-7 Prayer and asked them their names and where they were from. They told the girls that they were beautiful and asked how they could pray for them. Love, good lives, happiness – those were the things the girls most desired.

Even as they talked about their hopes and dreams – their prayers to God – another girl came out of a ticket booth, followed by a man pulling up his zip. She came and joined the group and they prayed together, that no matter what happened in their lives they would know God as their Father.

Elsewhere, Dave and Kim bumped into another group of girls – they too chatted and offered to pray. But as they were about to start, one girl interrupted saying, 'The name I told you is not my real name – this is my name ...' I guess she wanted to be sure that if someone was praying to God for her, God should know who was really being prayed for. 'That's a beautiful name', Dave said. We think that Dave's simple choice of phrase powerfully conveyed just a small part of what her Father God would say to her. That phrase was a heavenly response, a prophetic utterance through one of God's servants to an earthly, needy prostitute.

On another night, I went out with Anna and we bought white roses from the elderly Spanish rose sellers and gave them to yet another group of girls – telling them, 'God thinks you are beautiful'. It's all I could say. I think if I had tried to say any more I would have just cried.

For me these interactions were 'Psalm 139 moments'. We were calling their beauty out of them, expressing to them that God had smiled when he created them, and that he saw them as beauties even if the world we work in viewed them as commodities.

Just a few days after these interactions out on the streets, two of the ladies came in to our centre. They greeted our team with hugs, saying they had popped in because they had promised they would.

It seemed that God had pushed the door open a little bit.

I wish I could write now that we have been inundated with girls asking God to change their lives, and that we've seen hundreds of girls leaving a life of prostitution. Yet each year, there seem to be more and more of these girls working as prostitutes in San Antonio.

We would see men in pairs trying to negotiate a 'two for the price of one' deal, then standing there grinning at each other while two girls serviced them. Three doors away from our centre there was a boarded-up shop with a convenient doorway that was often used for business. Girls would disappear with lads behind wheelie bins, into dark apartment block doorways, into unlit car parks. Lads who looked like they were just out of school paid for these services, as well as guys in their twenties, thirties, forties, fifties ...

Some appeared too drunk to know what they were doing and were led off by girls desperate for business. Sometimes in their drunkenness, they misunderstand the situation – they might think they had 'pulled' for the night and after the deed was done, they would hang around trying to get close to the girl again, not realising that this was a business transaction that they had paid for. Some girls took advantage of the muddled state of guys – it seems it's quite easy to lift a wallet from the pockets of jeans or shorts when you're being paid for your hands and face to be in that general area.

From time to time, we would notice that all of the girls had disappeared – then shortly after we would spot a police patrol. Other times, the lookouts were not quite so alert and all you could do was watch helplessly as the girls fled, pursued by police either on foot or motorbikes. Sadly, you might see those same girls the next day with wheals, bruises and even broken bones.

It touches your heart to see and hear these things, but there is nothing romantic about it – this was not *Pretty Woman*!

Over the winter of 2008–9 we stumbled across – or more likely God led us to – a new understanding of the plight of some of these girls. It shocked us and broke our hearts.

We learned that there are many women in Europe working as prostitutes, many of them young girls trafficked from their home towns. Caught in poverty with no perceived hope of improving their lot, the offer of a better life in Europe is an attractive option. Such an offer coming from someone known, although not necessarily a close friend, carries a ring of authenticity. With the promise of domestic work and good earnings – sufficient to live on as well as send back to a needy family in Africa – girls set off with high hopes and dreams. They hope that one day, when they have all their European paperwork, they might even be able to bring more of their family over and help them get established in Europe too. It's not until they arrive in Europe that they discover that they owe their 'sponsors' huge amounts of money, and learn the true nature of how they will earn that money.

Maybe it was naïve of us but, until then, it hadn't crossed our minds that this could be the story of some of the girls we had met. We were overwhelmed as we realised that the problem was so much bigger and scarier than we had imagined. How could we even begin to respond to that? It's one thing to believe that maybe a girl would respond to God and make a decision to change her lifestyle – maybe we might even be able to help her with that. Somehow it seems a much bigger miracle to pray that she would be released from those who held her in debt bondage. And yet we still prayed that God would come and work miracles and help us as we made ourselves available to be involved in that.

At the start of the 2009 summer season, we picked up with the girls right from where we finished at the end of 2008. In the light of all we had learned, we were more resolved than ever to take every opportunity that God gave us to show love to these ladies.

One afternoon three girls called into our centre – some of the girls on our team had met them the previous evening. They wanted to use our prayer room for prayer. They asked if they could have ten minutes alone in there and then asked Christine and myself to go in and pray with them.

Kneeling with the girls, we called down the blessing of God on their lives. It's a strange world you live in when you find yourself kneeling in prayer with three prostitutes at 4.30 on a Tuesday afternoon – but at that point, there was nowhere else Christine and I would rather have been. The girls asked for full versions of the Bible. They didn't like the idea of our pink and yellow *Message* New Testaments: they preferred good old fashioned black HOLY BIBLES! Which we were delighted to be able to give them. We wrote messages in the front.

About three minutes later, five of their friends walked in, also wanting prayer and Bibles. After more prayer, the last remaining

Bibles in the centre were given to them. They promised to return the next day and asked if Christine would read the Bible with them when they came back.

It was a strange sight to see all these women leaving the centre, walking along the street with Bibles tucked under their arms. I'm sure God was smiling!

The girls began to come in regularly. When they first introduced themselves, they would give their street name, but each time they wrote down their prayer requests, they would use their real names. Most often their prayers were for a different job, a different life; they also prayed for safety and for their families. Reading the Bible with them became something we did regularly. We had to get more copies of the Bible to give away.

Our minds struggled to cope as we had these beautiful God-times with the girls during the day and then saw them at work by night. One night a couple of them helped two of our team clean and bandage a guy who'd cut himself. Sometimes they would call us over to help someone who was drunk – we never knew whether they had been their customers first.

We would see them take hold of some young lad who was clearly the worse for wear. Sometimes we would intercept and lead him gently away – and yet we wondered if we were just prolonging the time the girls would spend in debt bondage by taking away a potential paying customer!

One night I was approached by a girl myself. Obviously I declined her services – but we did just tell her what we were about and what we did. Instead of asking for a Bible or prayer, she asked if we could give her condoms!

Now we wrestled with a new dilemma. Shouldn't they buy their own? Or shouldn't their pimps or madams buy them? If they wouldn't buy them, should we give them some anyway, to protect them and their customers? Would giving away condoms be perceived as condoning prostitution?

This was something on which we discovered other people had strong opinions both for and against. We decided that we would let mercy triumph over judgement, absorb the flak and buy them condoms. Eventually we were given quite a lot and also purchased some very cheap ones through eBay.

Soon we found ourselves regularly handing over both a Bible and a bag of condoms. We would kneel in prayer with girls in the afternoon – and the same girls would kneel later that night to perform a sex act.

What we remain convinced of is that God's love extends to these women. He sees them and he knows their stories. He's there when they kneel to pray and he is there when they kneel to give oral sex – I imagine that the latter breaks his heart.

In 2010, we continued to give away Bibles and condoms. We could barely keep up with the demand for Bibles. On one occasion Tracy stood with the last two Bibles in her hand in front of four girls each wanting one. It's the only time I've ever witnessed anyone fighting over a Bible!

From the beginning of that season we decided to put on a Sunday evening service. This was a direct response to the request of the girls towards the end of the previous year.

After five weeks of the services being attended solely by our team, Tracy and I fought back tears as four girls walked into the service just as we had begun to sing. Five seasons of persevering in prayer and then you find yourselves sitting in a room worshipping with these girls – it can be a little bit emotional. Word spread and it became normal to have six to ten, sometimes more, working prostitutes attending our services, along with other seasonal workers.

To be honest, conversation could be awkward. The girls were not naturally relaxed at making small talk and we found ourselves struggling to find new things to ask about. The usual, 'How's work going?' – always a good opener with anyone else – just didn't feel appropriate. And sometimes it seemed that they didn't have much of a life outside of their work. Asking about their life in Spain was a bit of a minefield anyway as many of them were there illegally. We asked about their families, their homes in Africa, complimented them on their hairstyles and their earrings. We probably understood more about their lives by how they asked us to pray.

These girls loved to sing and loved to laugh. Each was someone's daughter, sister, friend. Some were mothers. We reminded ourselves that not one of these girls ever thought, 'When I grow up I want to be a prostitute'. Whatever their story, not one of them carried that as a childhood dream.

They kept calling into the centre, still asking for condoms and prayer, but some staying to chat. We set them up with Facebook accounts, laughed with them as they giggled helplessly at their own efforts to play table tennis and Mario Karts on the Wii. We included them in our offer of hand, feet and head massages that we had started to put on for female workers.

And that brings me back to Angel ...

We got to know Angel a bit more than any of the others. It stemmed from her love of singing and worship. In Poppy and Claire she found two great singers who were more than happy to sing their hearts out with her in the prayer room. And one day we got to hear her story ...

It was a story told with great sadness. When we asked her to clarify a few things later on, she asked not to talk about it any more because it made her feel too sad to think about it.

A few years previously, Angel had a son with her partner back in Nigeria. Her partner left her and as a single parent, she struggled to bring up her son alone. Work was hard to find – Angel had fallen on hard times, unable to feed and care for her son properly.

And then an old schoolmate contacted her – not a great friend, but someone she knew – and offered her the chance to come to Europe.

She told Angel that she and her friends could help her to get to Europe and then arrange domestic work for her: childcare, cooking or cleaning. So in 2006, Angel left her four-year-old son with his grandmother and came to Spain, hoping that she would be able to provide for her son and eventually bring him over to Spain too, where they could enjoy a better life together.

It wasn't until she arrived in Spain that she was told that she had incurred a debt for her transportation of €45,000 that she had to pay back to the people who had brought her over. And then she found out what she was expected to do to earn that money.

She spent the first months locked up in a room, and eventually was sent out to work. When we met her, she had been doing that for almost four years and had calculated that she might be able to pay off her debt after one more year.

She told us that her story was not as bad as some of the other girls she knew – some of them owed more money, some were made to swear oaths with priests in *juju* temples and lived with the fear that if they didn't repay their debt, the priests would be contacted and not only the girls themselves but their families too would be cursed with sickness or even death. The spiritual hold on those girls was stronger than we can imagine – and more than enough that making a run for it and trying to escape wasn't really an option.

Angel longed for a different life – she had tried to learn new skills so that when her debt was paid, she might be able to get legal work in Spain and be given resident status. And so then, maybe, that better life for her and her son could finally begin.

When she left Ibiza that summer, she was still in debt bondage – and yet she could still wholeheartedly sing of her love for her Saviour and King.

I don't know the full story of what happened to Angel after that, but I do know that she didn't return to Ibiza. We received a message from her that autumn saying, 'I have committed to fully follow Christ'. This was wonderful news. It became clear that somehow she was now free of prostitution, free of debt bondage and engaged to someone who also loves Jesus. They got married the following summer.

We have also heard the stories of one or two other girls – and snippets of a few more. Not everyone's story is the same as Angel's but the common thread is one of desperation, a lack of other options, and hopelessness.

We know that these girls are the most despised of all the people in and around the West End, scorned it seems everywhere, except amongst themselves and our team. They are used by men – and condemned for it too. Their sometimes aggressive pursuit of customers, and their reputation for robbing them, does not help their case.

We continue to pray for and with the girls – to offer them a welcome and friendship and generally seek to show, through our actions, the grace and mercy of a God who loves them and longs to see their lives changed even more than we do. A God who thinks they are beautiful.

We are often drawn to Christ's story of the two sons where, at the end of the Gospel of Matthew, 'Jesus said to them, "Truly I tell you, the tax collectors and the prostitutes are entering the kingdom of God ahead of you. For John came to you to show you the way of righteousness, and you did not believe him, but the tax-collectors and the prostitutes did. And even after you saw this, you did not repent and believe him'" (Matthew 21:31–32).

Christ knew there was room for prostitutes to enter his kingdom. We explored that. We allowed the girls primarily to belong, to be part of community, to find love and acceptance, to get to know them as individuals, not just lump them into a category of people in our minds who were different to us and from whom we kept our distance.

It was complex: people are. But I do believe that we should be willing to live with the complexity and the danger of being misunderstood for the sake of the gospel. Jesus was called a drunkard and a glutton, charges aimed at him because of the company he kept. A simple question to ask would be, 'When was the last time your reputation was called to account because of the company you keep?'

We had to remain patient and persistent. We had some beautiful moments with a few girls, and even saw some amazing answers to prayer for individual girls. We're really thankful that God has made a huge difference to one or two that we know of – and yet it's still not enough. Because there remain hundreds of girls still trapped in that life – for all sorts of reasons – we are jealous for more.

Breakthrough will come. But sometimes it will only come when we are persistent, when we don't stop and don't give up. It is overwhelming and I am sure there are other things people could do. But our hearts have to remain soft and we have to keep praying even in the face of insurmountable odds – and then, every now and again, we see an angel getting set free.

DON'T GIVE UP 10

I don't know why but today I have felt a weary emptiness. I was sitting by the kebab shop a few hours ago watching two Scottish guys haggle with a prostitute to see if she would do a 'two for the price of one' deal.

It just wears you out.

Tonight I witnessed quite a few drug deals. Ben was out and he saw a man put five lines of coke out on a table in open view of everyone and just start snorting.

This is a beautiful island and I don't want to misrepresent it – natural beauty, creative excellence, fantastic place for families to come on holiday, beautiful clubs, superb music and loads of sunshine.

But it still makes me weary.

Dawn and I have just spent the last hour with a girl getting her back to her hotel. Her friends had abandoned her, she puked all over the inside of the van, totally missing our bucket. When we pulled up at the hotel, a taxi driver called me a *puta* which isn't very nice – but he would never have taken her home: they don't do puking drunks. I didn't have time to get out and explain, but it just cut into me a little: here we are trying to help, and some guy is swearing at me because he thinks I am stealing his business.

After much stress – and loads of help from a porter and security guard – we get this girl out and along come her friends who had abandoned her. The first thing they did was take a photograph – can you believe that? We left her with them and then came back, and for fifteen minutes we cleaned the van out as by the morning it would stink.

So now I am weary.

I'll be okay. I just need God's heart to bleed into my heart, then I'll be fine.

Galatians 6:9, 'Let us not become weary in doing good, for at the proper time we will reap a harvest if we do not give up.'

The sun's coming up and cockerels are crowing so I should get to bed; my back hurts which isn't helping my sleep, and is probably contributing to my weariness.

I'm fed up with 'victorious Christian living'. I am victorious – he has given me victory over death and sin, he has given me so much. But a lot of the time I don't feel victorious. I feel desperate, I struggle and am tired.

I sometimes think 'You shouldn't say that Brian, you're admitting defeat.' Right now, I don't care. I AM WEAK.

I am weak, but I am not going to give up. I am going to overcome. I am going to persevere. I may not feel victorious, but I am not going to let go of God. This is an attitude of mind that we need to carry throughout our whole Christian life.

There are many times when I feel dirty, fearful, hurting and desperate – but I will hang on, I will overcome. I mightn't finish standing in a three piece suit looking like some sort of superstar: I might just finish panting, lying on the ground, covered in dust and sweat and hurting – but I will overcome.

I'm going to hang on.

I've been struck by the phrase 'Don't let go.'

Here's the deal: despite my present reality, which I mustn't ignore or pretend doesn't exist, I have to say to myself, 'Don't let go.'

I'm tired. Don't let go.

I've been praying for years. Don't let go.

This isn't easy. Don't let go.

I'm hurt. Don't let go.

I'm a mess. Don't let go.

I think this was 2007. I got in one morning around five, and wrote my blog while I tried to unwind. I was feeling weary, and, if I'm honest, a little sorry for myself. We had just started with our fourth two-week team and life was hectic – managing a team, dealing with the late nights and just trying to get time with the family. We had seven extra people, alongside our permanent team, working out on the streets. More people means spotting more situations, getting involved in more mess, dealing with more trauma and witnessing more madness.

I hoped I wouldn't give up. Christ didn't give up on me; he doesn't give up on us. And his body, the church, people I know in the church – they didn't give up on me. My father is the best example I know of this kind of christlikeness. He never gave up on me, never once. He may have struggled with my choices, he may have despaired as I slipped away from church, he may have found it hard to articulate his pain in seeing me go through dark days. But he never gave up on me.

His example – and my subsequent return to faith – has always stood at the back of my own personal history, as a reminder that I mustn't give up, even when it seems hope has gone and all is not well. Then I look at others who stood by me, visited me in prison, wrote me letters, prayed for me – Andrea who prayed for me for twenty years and never gave up on me, Robb and Sally who have stood by me since I was fifteen, never giving up on me – I hope I will never give up.

PERSEVERING IN THE BIBLE

That day, after my exhausted 'Don't let go' prayer, I rallied myself and went to bed feeling like *Braveheart*! There's truth in my exhausted rant – it does help to be honest with God. When I read it back, it seems like a mixture of prayer and me speaking to my own soul, a bit like David,

> Why, my soul, are you downcast?
> Why so disturbed within me?
> Put your hope in God,
> for I will yet praise Him,
> my Saviour and my God
>
> Psalm 42:5

David had been anointed to become King, but for years he was on the run from Saul – fleeing for his life, yet never allowing himself to lay a hand on him, because Saul was still God's anointed. David knew about persevering in the face of difficulty, and wrote many psalms about it. And there are countless other examples in the Bible encouraging us not to give up. The writer of Hebrews lists the heroes of the Old Testament and then encourages us, 'Therefore, since we are surrounded by such a great cloud of witnesses, let us throw off everything that hinders and the sin that so easily entangles. And let us run with perseverance the race marked out for us,' (Hebrews 12:1); Paul likens it to a race, saying 'Every athlete exercises self-control' and we should 'run so as to obtain the prize' (1 Corinthians 9:24, 25 ESV).

But it's from the story of Jacob I really get that sense of keeping on keeping on. Of overcoming, not giving up. Like Jacob wrestling with the angel saying, 'I will not let go.'

> That night Jacob got up and took his two wives, his two female servants and his eleven sons and crossed the ford of the Jabbok. After he had sent them across the stream, he sent over all his possessions. So Jacob was left alone, and a man wrestled with him till daybreak. When the man saw that he could not overpower him, he touched the socket of Jacob's hip so that his hip was wrenched as he wrestled with the man. Then the man said, 'Let me go, for it is daybreak.'
> But Jacob replied, 'I will not let you go unless you bless me.'
> The man asked him, 'What is your name?'
> 'Jacob,' he answered.
> Then the man said, 'Your name will no longer be Jacob, but Israel, because you have struggled with God and with humans and have overcome.'
>
> Genesis 32:22–28

I look at Jacob and as I think about him not letting go, I notice that he gets a name change – and I think, this wrestling, this holding on, affects our identity. It changes us inside. I also notice that he leaves the encounter with a limp – and I realise that this wrestling, this holding on, affects our walk. It affects the way we do things. There's an inner and outer change that happens to us when we dig deep and just hang on. My identity has been affected by persevering. And my walk has been affected by persevering.

Jacob persevered, in fact when I read about this man I see a certain tenacity that marks him as a man of perseverance. Jacob persevered to win his inheritance, persevered to win his wives, then wrestles with God. He sees God face to face and survives, and receives a blessing. He gets an identity change and walks differently. After this he is able to face his brother, and leave his past behind. After this he is able to purchase his very first piece of land, the promised land, and settle in Canaan.

When I look at the history of the church, I notice that often where there has been significant breakthrough or significant growth there are people who have been there a long time. People who have stuck it out through difficulty, who have persevered, who didn't give up, who eventually saw breakthrough. Most growing churches seem to have leaders who have been there a long time. Most healthy churches seem to have leaders who have been there a long time. So history tells me that breakthrough comes to those who stick at it.

> Every great story on the planet happened when someone decided not to give up, but kept going no matter what.
>
> *Spryte Loriano*

Up until a certain point, my moments of wanting to give up had been restricted to the occasional tired night or really crazy week, but then in 2009 we had a year of battling to not give up, a relentless ten-month emotional roller coaster of struggle! We had moved slightly out of town to a farm with a dream to use it as a place of refuge and retreat. Unfortunately it didn't work out: there were loads of practical challenges that, combined with the busy rhythm we were maintaining in the West End, threatened to overwhelm us. At one point we thought about leaving, about coming home. My nerves were frayed – I was snapping too quickly, trying too hard to hold it all together, Tracy was struggling emotionally – and we felt isolated and stretched beyond measure. TThat was when we learnt the most about perseverance: that tough time taught us more than the easy times.

Somehow we pulled through: after ten months we moved back from the farm, closer to town, and it was like someone flicked a switch – the work went to a new level, our flow and connectedness in the West End really grew. Right at the point when we felt most desperate, we held on; and when we got out the other end, God moved. For sure we limped and for sure it had affected our identity. At first we thought we had just failed but, looking back with that wonderful prophetic gift of hindsight, we see that this is where we learnt the most about perseverance.

ISAIAH 62

Somewhere along this journey, God drew us to Isaiah's prayer for Jerusalem. It was a call to us and it became our regular prayer for Ibiza. A clear theme of this prayer calls us not to give up.

Isaiah's Prayer for Jerusalem

Because I love Zion,

because my heart yearns for Jerusalem,
 I cannot remain silent.

I will not stop praying for her
 until her righteousness shines like the dawn,
 and her salvation blazes like a burning torch.

The nations will see your righteousness.
 World leaders will be blinded by your glory.

And you will be given a new name
 by the Lord's own mouth.

The Lord will hold you in his hand for all to see –
 a splendid crown in the hand of God.

Never again will you be called "The Forsaken City" or "The
 Desolate Land."

Your new name will be "The City of God's Delight"
 and "The Bride of God,"

for the Lord delights in you
 and will claim you as his bride.

Your children will commit themselves to you, O Jerusalem,
   just as a young man commits himself to his bride.

Then God will rejoice over you
   as a bridegroom rejoices over his bride.

O Jerusalem, I have posted watchmen on your walls;
   they will pray day and night, continually

Take no rest, all you who pray to the Lord.

Give the Lord no rest until he completes his work,
   until he makes Jerusalem the pride of the earth.

The Lord has sworn to Jerusalem by his own strength:
   "I will never again hand you over to your enemies.

Never again will foreign warriors come
   and take away your grain and new wine.

You raised the grain, and you will eat it,
   praising the Lord.

Within the courtyards of the Temple,
   you yourselves will drink the wine you have pressed."

Go out through the gates!
   Prepare the highway for my people to return!

Smooth out the road; pull out the boulders;
   raise a flag for all the nations to see.

The Lord has sent this message to every land:
   'Tell the people of Israel,

"Look, your Saviour is coming.
   See, he brings his reward with him as he comes."'

They will be called 'The Holy People'
   and 'The People Redeemed by the Lord.'

And Jerusalem will be known as 'The Desirable Place'
   and 'The City No Longer Forsaken.'

Isaiah 62:1–2 (NLT)

I hope I would never give up.

BUT HOW?

But it is easy to *feel* like giving up. Maybe I am just naturally pessimistic but I often feel like giving up – it is one of the biggest battles I face when it comes to prayer. If I don't see breakthrough, if I don't get the hoped-for results, I can get a little maudlin and be tempted to give up.

In Ibiza, it was often just the massive scale of the problem. It would hit me that for every one that we helped and took home, there was always another who we couldn't help, another who might get raped or robbed or beaten up or knifed or just lost and stumbling in the middle of the road trying to get home. A bit like King Canute, it often felt like we were trying to stop the tide. But just occasionally God would give us a glimpse – like some of the stories of 'secret histories' in the next chapter – we would hear of an answer to prayer, or someone would write a 'Thank-you!' note.

For all the tough times, we would have many more beautiful moments of prayer and conversation with individuals out on the street. We learned the importance of thankfulness and reflecting on these encouragements. At times, it was just so easy to let our minds dwell on the desperate nature of the saddest situations we encountered, forgetting for a moment to be thankful for all the joyful moments we experienced. On one of their early visits to the island, Pete and Sammy Greig encouraged our team with this phrase from 1 Thessalonians 5:16–18:

> Rejoice always, pray continually, give thanks in all
> circumstances; for this is God's will for you in Christ Jesus.

This stuck with us – we often remembered it and we always tried to communicate the importance of thankfulness to future teams.

Sometimes it was financial challenges: we could let the worry get to us, worries about finding the money for rent and bills and just to keep the work going. When we first signed the lease on the premises, because of my poor Spanish, I misunderstood the terms as we went to receive the key and hand over the deposit, we discovered that we were expected to pay a full year's rent up front, not just one month. Despondent, we left empty handed, feeling slightly sick. But, just as he did so many other times, God made a way. We learned to recollect those times, to be thankful and to trust him. As the stories of provision mounted up, they became like a reservoir to draw on when new challenges came along.

> Only be careful, and watch yourselves closely so that you do not forget the things your eyes have seen or let them fade from your heart as long as you live. Teach them to your children and to their children after them.
>
> Deuteronomy 4:9

We didn't let the good that God had done fade from our hearts!

Sometimes it was tensions in relationships. We were always under pressure with the late nights and tiredness, and the difficult situations and upsetting sights we saw. We recognised that it was all too easy for tiredness and stress to affect the way we were with each other within the team – snappiness, abruptness, letting trivial things build into a big deal – these things can add to the feeling of weariness and make you feel like giving up. We were never perfect! But becoming aware of these things, and consciously addressing them as a team, helped us to be more of an encouragement to each other than cause weariness in each other.

Community

When it comes to not giving up, it helps to be part of a community. Community is the essence and motivator that keeps us standing with one another in that moment when one of us needs extra encouragement not to give up. I guess in all that we talk about, we do have to remember that mission really does happen best in the context of community. Many nights have been mad, hectic and overwhelming – but we were never alone. When we are called to persevere in prayer it *can* seem mad, hectic and overwhelming, whatever the circumstance – but if *it's* in community that we face these challenges, then *it's* easier!

Bruce Gardiner Crehan and Helen Gross were with us for several years and were a blessing to us in so many ways. They helped to carry responsibility, they loved our boys, they noticed when we were struggling, they protected us, they saw us at our best – and at our worst – and they stuck it out. We prayed together, ate together, laughed together, cried together, even took a holiday together. It sounds perfect, but we did have some tensions! The thing is, through it all, these two went the extra mile and without them, there is so much that just would never have happened. You need people like that.

We were encouraged by the local Anglican church who supported us, shared meals with us and prayed for us. Spanish friends like Julia, Sara, Laia, Lupe and Raul who shared music, food and fun with us and put up with my random Spanish. All these guys kept us going. I'm constantly drawn back to the fact that without others we just won't make it. I don't know how anyone could work out the call of God on their life, or the need to see change in the world, on their own. Isolation is no help when it comes to persevering: we need others.

And we had churches in the UK who supported us, prayed for us, sent us gifts. This all contributed.

Beyond this, we realised how much we needed the support from back home – the beautiful relationships with our friends – Pete and Sammy, Ian, Billy and Caroline, Stevie and Catherine, Adrian and Jenny, Alain, Graham and Michele, Albert and Ange, the 24-7 leadership team – who called regularly and encouraged us. They would ring us – I think once Pete ran up a £40 bill on one call, he just knew how much I needed support at that particular time and forgot that he was on a mobile. We relied so much on the phone and the Internet to feel connected with friends and strengthened simply by talking things over with them for communication and also the visits.

Then I think about my marriage. At different times we have both talked each other away from the edge of giving up – Tracy has never let me give up and I have never let her give up.

> Two are better than one,
>   because they have a good return for their labour:
> If either of them falls down,
>   one can help the other up.
>
> Ecclesiates 4: 9–10

Families can be a blessing too – our wider families were always incredibly supportive, encouraging us with their visits and phone calls – sisters, brothers, parents, grandparents – we were blessed with good family relationships.

And most importantly we had the Lord – we had prayer and the word and worship. We needed continually to hear what God was saying, share our frustrations and lift him up. It was intense but, with everything else in place, we persevered.

PRAYER

Intimacy – The art of stillness

I have learnt that I need to cultivate the art of stillness. I need it even more when I am busy and persevering and pushing through.

Do you ever get that sense that there is something that lies just beyond your grasp? You're not even too sure what it is, a bit like a dream you had that you can't remember, but you know you had it. I sometimes feel like this in my quiet time – there's more than I am experiencing yet I just can't get to that place of inner stillness to truly feel it. I am so caught up in what I am doing and working for, that I have what I could only describe as restless prayer times! I withdraw – I make sure I go to the place of prayer with every intention to be still and meditative – but my mind gets crowded. This affects my stillness.

Sometimes I can achieve stillness more easily when engaged in a physical activity. A walk helps me to empty myself – I concentrate on the repetitive nature of plodding along and somehow I feel stiller. I do enjoy travelling alone and sometimes on a plane or in an airport I hear more, feel more and see more. Yet it is not enough. I sometimes like the idea of being a hermit, but I would get bored. I am an activist – I like being with people, I prefer wrestling to sitting knitting.

If I am going to live a truly missional life and see change happen, I need to be still as well as busy.

God calls us to 'Be still, and know that I am God' (Psalm 46:10), but quite often I am not very still and try to be God myself. And then elsewhere in the Bible, we are called to pray and give ourselves no rest (Isaiah 62:6). How can the two work together?

When we become serious about carrying Christ to the world and seeing our communities transformed by him, we need to perform a fine balancing act of of dealing with the paradox of stillness and activity.

Stillness is a mystery, a puzzle, maybe a lifelong quest. It is about getting into a place of connection with God that is less about what I do, and more about who I am. It's the journey of somehow trying to get my head around the omnipotent, omniscient, omnipresent, immutable, eternal being that is God. Can't think I will ever have that sorted but stillness is where I try to contemplate these things! And, as I contemplate them, they seem to help me in my perseverance.

I know so little about him, not even the tip of the tip of the iceberg of who he is.

I like that – the mystery, the constant journey, the sense that God will always be just out of reach, close yet far, intimate yet distant, in me yet out there, revealed yet hidden, audible yet silent. I get all of this when I enter a place of stillness.

In the early days, when we prayed before we went out on the streets, we would often sound a bit hyped up. Our prayers would be loud, frantic and desperate, maybe a bit nervous! We learned that a period of stillness before going out was incredibly helpful – less crashing the gates of hell and more sitting on God's lap.

How do we cultivate stillness?

Do we enter the place of a prayer in a hurry? Do we rush it as part of a daily routine, quickly say what we need to say, then finish?

The psalmist writes: 'I have calmed and quieted myself, I am like a weaned child with its mother; like a weaned child I am content' (Psalm 131:2).

Not only in times of prayer, but in life generally, we need to grow in stillness. In a world that is fast moving and full of noise we need to learn how to withdraw into God and find peace and stillness in him.

One of our 24-7 Boiler Room leaders in the UK, Sally Harman, once said, 'We have learned to do less and pray more.' How does that statement make you feel? I like it: when we decide to do less and pray more we recharge, are re-energised and gain fresh momentum for the journey.

Living in a place of outstanding beauty also helped us to keep going. I didn't articulate it this way at the time but in hindsight I think I had begun to practice a spirituality of wonder. Which was another thing that helped me to keep going. I would walk the dog every day, next to the Mediterranean Sea. I would take time to appreciate the sky, the waves, the breeze, the natural erosion of the rocks, the hills in the background, the birds soaring – they would all feed me, remind me of my Creator, lift my spirits and keep me going. A spirituality of wonder helped me to be still but also helped me to persevere.

I love this description from the late Brennan Manning:

> We get so preoccupied with ourselves, the words we speak, the plans and projects we conceive that we become immune to the glory of creation. We barely notice the cloud passing over the moon or the dewdrops clinging to the rose leaves. The ice on the pond comes and goes. The wild blackberries ripen and wither. The blackbird nests outside our bedroom window. We don't see her. We avoid the cold and the heat. We refrigerate ourselves in the summer and entomb ourselves in plastic in winter. We rake up every leaf as fast as it falls. We are so accustomed to buying pre-packaged meats and fish and fowl in supermarkets we never think and blink about the bounty of God's creation. We grow complacent and lead practical lives. We miss the experience of awe, reverence, and wonder.[1]

I learned to stop for a minute, look up and experience the world with awe, reverence and wonder.

This chapter could sound a bit intense – we also learned to have a family and community life outside of the work. At the busiest times, this meant carving out chunks of time for us to be just the four of us as a family. I developed some nice personal rhythms of meeting with friends to play backgammon, walking the dog and swimming in the sea. As a team we planned some exclusive times just to relax together, which meant we didn't invite any guests or

---

[1] *The Ragamuffin Gospel*, Brennan Manning (Multnomah 1990).

anyone we worked with. We just hung out together, ate together, went to the beach together or played games together. Generally we tried to build a sense of closeness and support.

Persevering is about good personal care and also good pastoral care. We programmed our work so that everyone had nights off and if they ever felt too tired, we would do our best to give people extra breaks. We met with every member of the longer term team individually every two weeks to ensure that they were processing everything they saw in a helpful way. It was an opportunity for the individual to talk about what they were learning – what was a struggle, what they were really enjoying, what they were feeling. We also tried to give them encouragement and feedback that would be helpful for their time with us – and, we hoped, beyond. If trauma or other scenes were witnessed, we would talk about that and had friends back in the UK we could refer people to. On top of this, everyone had church contacts and home support. All our teams also met in smaller groups with each other and asked good accountability questions of one another. Tracy and I did the same. This all helps when it comes to persevering.

Sometimes you don't give up because you have people cheering you on. We had friends who phoned, people who visited, who let us unwind and debrief: we can't underestimate how much this helped us to keep going.

PRAYING IN COMMUNITY

I know of one big church which is trying to ensure that their people are never more than twenty-four hours away from the opportunity to participate in an organised prayer event of some shape or form. They are building prayer into the life of the church. There is a responsibility for us to have our own personal, disciplined, responsible prayer lives, but when you are part of a community that places high value on prayer it cannot help but affect you. The macro affects the micro and *vice versa*. Persevering is easier with friends!

I think the popularity of 24-7 Prayer has come about because it has given the body of Christ a tool which they can take, shape and adapt to fit their particular local setting, which facilitates and encourages community. It helps the church to pray.

Of course it is not the only way – and really our heart is not on selling a model, but it is on people and communities praying. I don't care if you never have a 24-7 Prayer room. I care that as a community you pray and you persevere together.

A healthy community will have a healthy corporate prayer life but will also be full of people who have healthy personal prayer lives. People who are persevering privately are great to have on board when you are persevering corporately!

Healthy communities and churches will have healthy prayer lives, which in turn should all help in not giving up.

Don't give up.

Prayer check

Here are few simple ideas, a few questions to ask yourself and reflect on which might help you to keep going, and to not give up. They are not meant to patronise you and this is not a comprehensive list, but I find them helpful.

- *Do you set regular time aside every day to pray?* Pete Greig says that a remote control and an alarm clock would be your most useful tools in this. I would also hasten to add the 'off' button on your computer, iPad or smart phone. I read this recently, written by a social scientist: 'What information consumes is obvious: it consumes the attention of its recipients. Hence a wealth of information creates a poverty of attention.'[1] I am constantly having my attention consumed, constantly being drawn away from being attentive to God by my laptop!

- *Do you fast?* Jesus did. Start small, but at some point you should be looking to do three days without food. There is something about fasting that seems to help – perhaps it focuses us on the prayer, perhaps it helps us realise we're serious, but it does seem to bring breakthrough.

- *Do you practice petition and perseverance?* Write your prayers down, keep a notebook, don't give up! Don't let the instant culture we live in shape us. And every now and then, read back over your notebook. You will be amazed at the answers.

- *Are you thankful?* Remember to take the time to appreciate what is good in your life – and be thankful.

- *Are you actively trying to grow your prayer life?* Read about prayer, educate yourself, learn from others. This will all help you.

- *Are you praying with others?* Get to prayer events. Attend prayer meetings, pray with others whenever you can.

- *Are you making time to withdraw and be with God?* Get to a 24-7 Prayer room or go on a mini retreat. Participating in a week of prayer is wonderful – spending an hour, contemplating, painting, writing, talking or ranting on your own. This is of immense value. But a word of caution: it can be a very individual and quiet time. Often we have to be careful this does cause us to lose the ability to pray out loud with others. There is power in the prayer of agreement – I can't agree with you if I can't hear you!

- *Is your prayer life accountable to anyone?* Do you have a friend who can ask you how your prayer life is going, who will encourage you to run and not give up?

- *Ask God to help you, to let you see some of the results of your prayer.* It was a great encouragement to us – see the next chapter, 'Secret Histories'.

Our Father in heaven,
  may your name be kept holy.
May your Kingdom come soon.
May your will be done on earth,
  as it is in heaven.
Give us today the food we need,
and forgive us our sins,
  as we have forgiven those who sin against us.
And don't let us yield to temptation,
  but rescue us from the evil one.

Matthew 6:9-13 (NLT)

SECRET HISTORIES

SECRET HISTORIES 11

First night back on the streets as a street pastor since Ibiza and I met a guy called Steve in Falmouth town … who Carolyn and I helped when we were in Ibiza!! Thought I recognised him but not from Ibiza. He just happened to mention how he was in Ibiza and how two people helped his friend in a wheelchair and it all suddenly clicked! Both of us suddenly recognised each other! We helped his friend back to her room at Ibiza Rocks Hotel in a wheelchair and gave him a 'Jesus Loves Ibiza' Bible! The thing is he doesn't even come from Falmouth; only God can plan things like that!!! Steve in his own words said 'God is following me!', 'I'm just mind blown' and how it was 'the highlight of his night'. Certainly no coincidence! I'm just floored, only our God can do things like that, He's so awesome. (e-mail 02.10.11)

hey guys,

just thought i wud encourage you's with something that happened this morning

i dont know if any of you remember during our team in the summer i met people from ballynahinch who i knew. and one of the girls i knew – sarah, cause i worked with her. well this morning as i was driving into church, i seen sarah walk past – she was going into church!! as i got in, i looked for her, and seen she was sitting right in front of me-flipping rite!! i got chatting to her for a bit-it was so good! she went home really quickly after the service, so i didnt get talking to her. but keep praying for her – its brilliant she was there!!!!!!!!!!!! God's still working – keep praying for those who we met this summer! hope you are all well!" (fb msg October 25 2009)

Another team member replied:

> Wohooo mentally good times!
>
> To add to the whole 'God is still working through the people we met in Ibiza' Do you remember the guy I met in Ibiza called Nick (on the sunset strip and who lives in Scarborough)??! well he got in touch yesterday and wants to meet sometime this week to talk about all things good. woop! Pray that it will be an amazing God conversation.
>
> love and blessings

Then another replied:

> While we're on the subject my mate in Toulouse called Carl worked at sunset strip in Savannah (i think) and he used to come into 24-7 room all the time. so would be great if you could pray for him, he absolutely loved what 24-7 do and what they stand for, he only had good things to say hope thats an encouragement
>
> October 26, 2009

Most people we helped we didn't hear from again – we had no idea what happened to them. But sometimes it was as if God wanted to give us a glimpse into what he was doing beyond and through our work in Ibiza. It was the most exciting thing.

One day I had a really random phone call from a guy who was camping on the island: *'Hi, my name is Jack. I have just become a Christian and would like to be baptised. Do you do that sort of thing?'* I quickly asked him how it had happened and he said, *'I have been looking at the beauty of this island and decided that something this beautiful had to be created and that there has to be a God, so I decided to become a Christian, I checked out online what I needed to do and have made the choice.'* It was a wonderfully surreal moment. We met up and talked – and he had indeed found Jesus, so we had the privilege of baptising him in the Mediterranean Sea.

God was at work with us and without us. People were continuing to be impacted by our work – by God – after returning home. Complete strangers were being touched by God on their own, moved by creation. For years people had walked the island – our teams and no doubt others before them – asking that God would reveal himself to people in the beauty of creation. When we received messages with stories like these, we started to see that prayer really worked – that our prayers really worked. That they were effective. It was as if God was giving us a little glimpse, showing us that those prayers were not simply shots in the dark – that our prayers *are* 'powerful and effective' (James 5:16) – and that they are heard and answered.

I got to baptise Jack because people had sown this specific prayer into the island for years. Most who had prayed that prayer never got to see that great day when we baptised Jack, in fact there were only seven of us present. Other people's prayers had been effective – had caused a change in a man's life – but they knew nothing about it.

We had another phone call from a DJ in a major club who had become a Christian while on holiday in another country. Over the years we had sent teams to pray as they danced in that club, asking that God's light would shine in that place, that he would reveal himself to all involved in the creative club industry on the island, and we always prayed for the DJs. So did our prayers have something to do with his conversion? I like to think so! I'm sure we played a part.

Kris was a guy who connected with early 24-7 teams before we ever arrived on the island. He became a friend to us over the next few summers as he spent time with our family, shared meals with us and stayed in our home. Eventually he gave his life to Jesus and I got to baptise him. It would be easy for us to say that the reason he came to Christ was the great work 24-7 Prayer did in Ibiza: for sure we were part of the story, but the truth is his mother has prayed for him every day of his life. I believe the moment was hers. For every story that is told, there is another story that we don't see.

A while ago we had the privilege of listening to the wisdom of a wonderful man called Ken McCreavy, a friend of 24-7 Prayer and a highly respected church leader within the UK. Ken passed away not long afterwards. One of the statements that Ken made sticks in my mind and helps as we look at prayer and mission. He said *'For every history that is seen there is always a secret history, a history that is unseen.'* I really liked that. For every revival that breaks out, there is always a church or leader who goes down in history as the leader of the moment. Behind all of these I suspect that there were probably people who prayed for years for breakthrough in their town, or some ladies who prayed faithfully that God would bless and anoint their leader. For every history that is seen there is a secret, unseen history.

I love the fact that as we walk the streets and pray with people, we get to be involved in their secret history. That as we bump into people and have random encounters with people in all sorts of different social orbits, we can take those people on in prayer with faith. That if we pray for them constantly and consistently, stuff happens, whether we see it or not.

A friend of mine was in Amsterdam in the eighties. One day he was out with his girlfriend, they were smoking weed, and they stopped to listen to a band play. While they listened, a guy approached them, told them the band was a Christian band and offered to pray for them. They were very reticent and at first they refused. But he persisted and eventually they let him pray for them. He prayed – and then when he finished praying, my friend looked him in the eye and said, 'You see, it didn't work, nothing happened.'

I can only imagine that the poor guy who had prayed went home feeling pretty deflated, and probably didn't put that encounter in his latest update to his friends and supporters! Yet my friend went home and, amazingly, six months later through a whole set of circumstances, he and his girlfriend gave their lives to Jesus and still follow him to this day. That guy who first prayed for them knows nothing of this – and yet he too is involved in their secret history.

We live in a results-driven world: if we don't see results, we can feel that we have failed. Yet so often prayer is the long haul, or prayer is the secret place. When we pray with people, or for people, we get the opportunity to become involved in their secret history. We may never see the end result but when we pray, we have to trust that God is at work and that every time we pray something happens. We sow seeds in prayer that grow over time: sometimes we see the results, other times we don't – but because we don't see results doesn't mean nothing has happened.

I read this from an interview with the Spanish painter Joan Miró on his thoughts about surrealism:

> What counts more than the painting itself is what it exudes, what it spreads. Little matter if the painting is destroyed. Art

may die, but what is important is that it spreads its seeds on the soil. Surrealism pleased me because the surrealists did not regard painting as an end. A painting should not cause concern about remaining what it is, but rather that it should produce seeds, that it spreading sowings from which other things will grow ...

I think we can relate that to prayer and secret history – we can get overly concerned with the picture and forget that we are spreading seeds that we hope will grow in people's lives.

How do I pray into someone's life?

ON THE WALL

Every time we were able to pray with someone on the street, we believed it was an opportunity to connect that person with God himself, so we prayed in that moment with faith and earnestness. Often there would be a written prayer request which, with their permission, we would take back to the prayer room and pray over. If they had given permission for others to see it, we would pin it to the prayer room wall as a reminder to keep praying.

There were some people that we were seeing often and felt really moved by what came up in our team prayer times every week. We met others that we knew God was especially calling us to persevere in prayer for personally and we encouraged team members to make specific individuals part of their regular personal prayers. As we started to pray regularly for more and more people, it really helped to have a journal as a reminder. Have you ever promised to pray for someone then forgotten? Write it down and then look at what you have written on a regular basis.

For some years now, I've been keeping a book, writing people's names in it, and using it in my prayer times. I realised I would often say to people that I would pray for them but forget to do it. This meant I would end up offering up some bland prayer when they eventually entered my mind and I felt guilty for failing to do what I had said I would. Keeping a book reminds me and makes sure I do what I say I will do. This, or some other kind of prompting tool, helps when it comes to being deliberate about prayer. It means that when people ask you to pray for them, you keep your word, and you get to be a part in a secret history of connecting that person to God himself. You can say to people with assurance, 'I will pray for you.'

Over the years I have crafted prayers for individuals, added verses and thoughts on the page where their names are written in my book. So even if I am really tired I can read that prayer out again and focus on bringing a meaningful petition to God for that person. It's really helped me and I hope and trust has had a positive effect on those I've committed to pray for.

DIVINE HAUNTING

This is also where haunting comes into it! Now I know using the word 'haunting' sounds weird, but I use it in the sense of something continually coming back to mind, something unforgettable. It's very like when Paul warns the Ephesian believers not to lie to each other or stay angry with each other in case they 'give the devil a foothold' in the community (Ephesians 4:27). I believe that, every time someone agrees to let you pray for them, they give God permission, a way in to their lives, and I think of it as a foothold.

Once we had prayed with someone out on the street, that wasn't the end of it: we would pray for them again in the next prayer time back in the prayer room. We prayed that God would haunt them, that they would meet people who are Christians, that friends would find faith, that people at work would talk to them about the Lord, that they would have dreams about Jesus, that they would start to ask questions about their eternal security, that they would find a strange interest in the Bible, that they would start to see God in nature, that God would make them aware of his presence and love, that they would want to visit a church. Basically we prayed that God would haunt them. This was not a time for half-hearted or vague prayers – someone has given God a foothold, opened themselves to God just a little bit, and we wanted this to be just the start of it. There was a chink in their armour of resistance or disbelief the minute they agreed to be prayed for. We prayed that chink would widen and they would invite him in. We prayed with energy – this was no time for half measures. If we truly believed that knowing God would transform their lives in a positive way, we had to be serious and passionate in our prayers for them.

HEARTS AND SHOULDERS

It's actually an exciting thing that we get to participate in people's secret histories by prevailing in prayer. This praying, which is sometimes seen as the boring hard slog of the Christian life, has the potential to transform lives. Writing people's names on the prayer room wall, or in our journals, and consistently holding them up to the Lord in prayer, reminds me of a picture in Exodus:

> Engrave the names of the sons of Israel on the two stones, the way a gem cutter engraves a seal. Then mount the stones in gold filigree settings and fasten them on the shoulder pieces of the ephod as memorial stones for the sons of Israel. Aaron is to bear the names on his shoulders as a memorial before the Lord.
>
> Exodus 28:11, 12

I like that picture of Aaron carrying the people on his shoulders. We need to carry people on our shoulders in prayer. We need to carry them on our shoulders with strength and authority. But prayer is more than a duty – we need to feel it in our hearts as well. Later in the same chapter we are told:

> Whenever Aaron enters the Holy Place, he will bear the names of the sons of Israel over his heart on the breastpiece of decision as a continuing memorial before the Lord.
>
> Exodus 28:29

We need to have people over our hearts when we pray. We need to have something of God's compassion. As God grows our love for people, we pray more – and are given more to pray for! If we carry people on our hearts as well as our shoulders, it becomes a lifelong call.

When we really think about it, the things in our lives that mean the most to us, the secret of our successes and breakthroughs, is probably not solely down to our gifts and talents. These triumphs are probably also because someone, somewhere, has been praying for us. Someone has steeped us in prayer. Many a person who has accomplished great things has had people in the background praying.

Abraham Lincoln said 'I remember my mother's prayers and they have always followed me. They have clung to me all my life.' Here was a man who accomplished much – his mother's prayers clung to him his whole life. When we engage in prayer for others, we should do so with the hope and faith that the prayers we pray for them will cling to them for their entire lives.

My father tells me he has prayed for me every day of my life. That's quite humbling. I have always known he does and can't remember a time when he hasn't. He's an early riser; I don't think it's because he's naturally a morning person – it's primarily because he sets his alarm and gets up to pray! Actually, as he's committed to pray for more and more people, he finds himself having to get up increasingly earlier to get through them all. He's prayed for me through my dark days in prison and through my lighter years in church. It's probably one of the best things he has done for me. I do believe that my father's prayers have significantly affected me. His prayers haunt me – they cling to me – and I believe I am who I am today because he and others were willing to secretly pray.

Brennan Manning uses the phrase, 'I was seized by the power of a great affection' to describe being 'born again'.[1] It's a beautiful phrase. That is why I am who I am. Through the prayers of others, I have been seized by the power of a great affection. I feel his great affection, his great passion, his passion for me. His passion that my life should not be mediocre, his passion to see me become all I could be. His passion that allows me to be my raw unadulterated self. His passion that grips me, and drives me. His passion that is my crutch when I am weak. His passion that allows me to speak to him and tell him all that I am. His passion that sees all my weaknesses yet somehow still considers me worthy of his love.

I am weak, full of sin, slightly annoying, arrogant at times, lustful, deceitful, self-referenced, selfish, manipulative and angry.

---

[1] *The Ragamuffin Gospel*, Brennan Manning (Multnomah 1990).

Yet I have been seized by the power of a great affection and that absolutely amazes me.

An old Russian proverb says, 'Those who have the disease called Jesus will never be cured'. Please no one try and cure me. I am happy being infected by Christ. And because I love the way he wants to infect others, I will pray for that to happen, whether I get to see it for myself or not.

Be seized by the power of a great affection, let it drive you to pray that others would be infected.

For every history that is seen, there is a secret unseen history. For every story that is told, there is another story that we don't see.

DON GIOVANNI

We were sitting having our dinner one evening, when the phone rang. It was the Spanish doctor from the medical centre in San Antonio. A guy had been brought in who wasn't ill, but needed someone to talk to. Bethany and I went along and when we got there we found out the guy was Italian, so with Bethany's fluent Spanish – if you know a bit of Spanish you can understand a bit of Italian – we listened for over an hour to his sad tale.

Eventually, even though he didn't know we were Christians, he communicated that his problem wasn't physical it was spiritual! He told us that when he was low in the past his Italian priest prayed with him and he felt better – he even showed us how his priest prayed by placing his hand on his head. So we asked if we could pray for him. He said, '*Si!*' So I laid my hand on his head and prayed that God would bring him peace. It was amazing. His whole countenance changed, his shoulders lifted, his face became relaxed, a gentle smile appeared and his breathing became steady.

Then, in a gentle and steady voice, he asked to pray for us – first he kissed a picture of his priest five times, then we also had to kiss it. Then he prayed, in Italian. I have no idea what he said – although I could pick out '*Grazie Gesù!*' now and then. Then he stood up hugged and kissed us both and said in broken English, '*You people are from a different world.*' We walked him out and he left happy.

This is the simplest of stories, about God working in spite of us, in spite of language barriers and religious affiliation. God just showed up and was God. Bethany and I had the privilege to be part of this simple little story. But it just reminds me of God's great compassion and passion for man: that some slightly freaked-out, disturbed Italian guy in a hospital in San Antonio can move God so much that he sends along two random people who somehow get to be conduits for that guy's blessing. We will never see him again – but we got to be part of his secret history.

And then, just very occasionally, we get to hear a little more of someone's story, more than a message. God gives us a glimpse into what he is doing in people's lives. It encourages us to persevere, to keep going.

JAYNE'S STORY

There are moments in life that are special – marriages, new births, graduations, birthdays ... and then there are memories in life that can cut you to the core. A snapshot in time where 'special' just doesn't seem to cut it. A unique, stop-yourself moment that leaves you changed forever. My first encounter with the living Lord was one of them.

You see I was your average party girl. Summer 2012 was my third annual fortnightly holiday on the party island of Ibiza with a group of friends. Most people only visit San Antonio for a week, for many it's all they can handle but often we would shock other hotel residents that we were doing it for the two weeks. Hardcore. It was our escape from university, part-time jobs and the mundane realities of life. An opportunity for us to constantly let our hair down without a care in the world. Well, that was the pretence anyway.

In August of that year while the cocktails flowed, flirting with guys continued and we danced to sunrise, I remember feeling that for some reason I wasn't enjoying the trip as much as other years. And ten days in, when friends wanted to head to yet another globally famous all-nighter nightclub, I had to turn down the offer, opting to spend an evening watching an infamous Ibizan sunset alone, reflecting on my life.

Since I had arrived this year, something felt different. There was a hidden underlay of Ibiza in my heart. Although outwardly I would show it was amazing, Ibiza was actually a place where I would try to mentally block a lot of things. Every year it had robbed me more and more of my self-worth, sensibility and respect. I would self-meditate with things of the world, hoping that it would fill that hole that I had deep down felt for a long time.

Café Mambo and Café Del Mar were often hangouts of mine. I went off on my own out to the rocks hungover, wrecked, diminished. I purposely sat up away from the crowds as often thousands turn out to view it. By that stage I just craved silence. Peace. A peace that somehow I knew this place was ultimately never going to fill.

As I sat in silence, watching the sun pass further and further below the horizon, a surge of emotions ran through me. A beautiful vast ocean of the whole world glistening at my feet and I'm wasting, chasing after things that block all that out. A creation of sunset colouring, radiance and beauty that took my absolute breath away. I had seen this sunset before but often that was with a few drinks on a come down. Now I stared at it sober. Real. Consuming me further into its embrace. Suddenly I wasn't aware about anything else. Anyone else. Just lost in the awe at the wonder of creation. When I looked at this sunset, I realised given all my party years over the Mediterranean (which also included Magaluf, Ayia Napa, Marmaris to name but a few), I had never noticed how perfect a sunset could be. In fact I had never taken time to appreciate how pretty creation is – period. Is this all that I had made life to be – a whirlwind of endless parties, jobs and low self-esteem? Is this it?

I didn't vocalise anything. But my inner self cried a pang so deep that a response from the loving God Almighty was unstoppable.

I had heard people say, '"God told me this, God told me that,"' and always thought it was nonsense. I went to Sunday School as a little girl and I had no recollection of any so-called God speaking to me. Why had I not heard anything? In the next moment I discovered God had been with me my whole life – I had just never noticed. I didn't hear an audible voice. No: something much deeper. I became very aware of a warm spiritual presence around me, within me, beckoning me.

And instantly, right then, within me, like the change of skies, sunsets and mystery, I heard a voice: a still, small yet powerful voice respond deep within my heart. It said, '"Life is so much more than what your eyes are seeing. You will find your way if you start believing. Jayne, I have a plan for you more breathtaking than this sunset and I love you beyond comprehension."'

Overwhelmed, touched yet not fearful, I cried. It happened just as the sun went right down. With darkness beginning to loom and aware that I was alone, I made my way back to my hotel. My friends were all out and I got an early night. Three days later we flew home. Two weeks later I felt compelled to turn on the 'religion' section of Sky TV. With no Christian friends it was my only hope for some answers. And there on the screen was a band I had never heard of, the presenter just beginning to introduce 'Kutless' singing 'What faith can do.'

Some lines from the song are:

Life is so much more
Than what your eyes are seeing
You will find your way
If you keep believing

I looked at the screen with my heart pounding. Suddenly that warm peaceful presence came around me again. A peace that surpassed all understanding. And I knew God of the heavens and the earth, the Lord of Lords and King of Kings, had spoken to me – a nobody, a sinner, a fool. And He was going to show me life. Life to the full.

A year later I was helping a local church take a youth group to a local summer youth conference where Brian was speaking. God provided an opportunity for me to chat with him after and I learned that there was a 24-7 Ibiza team who went every night to the rocks to pray asking God to reveal Himself. I truly believe in the power of the prayer. I have no doubt in my mind that God chose that moment, that location, that mystery for me on the faithfulness of the team.

Since that time I have heard of people who have served with the Ibiza team and instantly my heart melts. Dedication to go into some of the biggest nightclubs in the world, surrounded by people trying to fill a void that only Jesus can, is not just 'good' – it is servanthood at its core. Having served on many international mission teams since, I am still floored at the love of a team to go out night after night in Ibiza! The perseverance, character and hope that they have are beyond inspiring. I may not always get it, but I praise God for it and I, for one, will be eternally grateful for 24-7 Prayer.

Jayne Booth
Northern Ireland

EPILOGUE

EPILOGUE

Our last year in Ibiza was challenging. But also incredibly rewarding.

In January 2012 we were invited to go to a meeting with others from the island, to talk about the British tourist drinking situation and to discuss a project for addressing the problems brought about by binge drinking. It so happened that the meeting was on my birthday. It was to be held at the offices of the British Vice Consul so Tracy and I assumed that it would be quite a large meeting. But when we got there, only the heads of various agencies were in attendance – and us! Somehow, as a movement, we had gone from being people who were stirred to pray when the British Vice Consul resigned in 1998, to being people invited to sit round the table at a consultation there fourteen years later. God is good. It was a great birthday present for me, and a wonderful testament to his faithfulness!

Then came Abby and Charlie. God had already shown us that our time in Ibiza was coming to an end and so we began to plan our move back to the UK, where I now head up 24-7 Prayer in Great Britain. But we didn't want the work to end, and, more importantly, we didn't feel God wanted the work to end. We had often thought of Abby and Charlie, a really wonderful couple who had both served on two-week teams and had recently married. Abby had also been with us for several months one summer. We felt God prompt us to invite them to come and lead the work, and they said yes. So early that year they moved out to work alongside us and we began the process of handing the work over to them.

God really knows what he is doing. They are a strong, creative, anointed couple with a set of skills that make them perfect for the job; they are compassionate, tenacious, thoughtful, prayerful and committed to pursuing whatever God leads them into. We couldn't have asked for better. They are there now, making it happen, taking the work further, developing a strong year-round community and continuing to shine in the West End of San Antonio.

Eventually our final week in Ibiza came. The team threw a surprise party for us, caught us completely off guard and really nailed it. As we entered the room there were lots of different people there and we got pretty emotional! One of the highlights for us was seeing the bar owners there, guys who had become our friends. And they presented us with a cake! Now the cake was important because of what it said on it.

Bear with me here – I am a great believer in regularly asking ourselves the question, 'If your church disappeared tomorrow, would the community you work in miss you?' During our time in Ibiza, we had developed a rhythm of team members being out on the streets six nights a week – we just couldn't physically cope with seven! Which brings us back to the cake. The bar owners had reproduced our logo in beautiful icing, except that it read '24–6 Ibiza!'

I was deeply moved by this gentle joke, because it spoke to me about the fact that when our team were absent, we were missed, when God's people weren't out on the streets, the people who worked on those streets noticed the difference. God somehow had inspired people to pray and to visit Ibiza, to pray and move out to Ibiza and in doing so he propelled 24-7 Prayer to become an integral part of the community it served. It was an honour to be involved in that chapter of his heart for Ibiza.

So that was our story. Really it's only part of a story.

The following week we sat and prepared for our last ever Sunday evening service in Ibiza, when in walked Sam. Sam was a worker who came to Ibiza the previous year to party and do what workers do; this year Sam had come as member of one of our two-week teams, because he found Jesus! This was the first time we had seen him since the last summer; he sat down to chat to us and one of the first things he said to us was, *'I am one of the fruits of the tree you guys planted'*.

What a particularly beautiful moment for our last Sunday!

Tracy and I took the service surrounded by friends: bar workers, teachers, tourists, prostitutes, summer workers, Spanish friends and residents, team members and our new leaders, Abby and Charlie. We felt an overwhelming sense that what had happened here had been good and that God had been faithful. We actually have been overwhelmed by God's goodness; a 'mantra' we are repeating a lot at the moment is *'God is good and his love endures forever'*.

The four of us arrived in Ibiza in March 2005. We didn't have a lot established – there was no centre and no grounded work. But there was a tremendous foundation of prayer. That foundation of prayer was what gave this work depth and set it up to grow. Many stood with us through the growth: from the first prayer room, to the Internet drop-in centre, the Vomit Van and wheelchairs, workers packs and *Jesus loves Ibiza* Bibles, lighters and condoms, and full Bibles for prostitutes. They stood with us as we developed strip club chaplains, massages for girls in prayer rooms, prayer requests on the streets, relationships with the health centre and local police, received encouragement from the British Consul and even the odd shout-out on Radio 1!

When I think back over those years, I am pretty convinced that lives have been changed. People have been prayed for and learned to pray themselves; people have been listened to; drunk and drugged people have been taken to safety; help and support has been given to people who have been injured, robbed and even raped; meals have been served; hospitality has been extended; people have been baptised; lives have been transformed. And it has been wonderful.

The beauty is that the work continues. It's bigger than us and God's relentless, unstoppable kingdom will continue to advance in Ibiza.

At our party where we received the cake, one of the bar owners thanked us on behalf of all 'The Westenders'. This touched us so deeply as we recalled the label once given to that area – Sodom and Gomorrah. We never saw it that way. Instead, this is what we pray for and believe about the West End, this is how we feel God sees it: 'Never again will you be called the Godforsaken City or the desolate land. Your new name will be the City of God's delight and the Bride of God, for the Lord delights in you and will claim you as His own' (Isaiah 62 NLT). This will continue to be our prayer of faith for San Antonio long after we have left.

All of this happened, and continues to happen, because of the 'passionate commitment of the Lord of Heaven's Armies' Isaiah 9:7 (NLT). 24-7 Prayer have joined in that commitment, sending early prayer teams to Ibiza and being willing to go to what people perceived as a dark place. We were blessed to have been sent there by them and supported and encouraged throughout. All that has happened so far is a beautiful example of prayer and mission working hand in hand and we feel privileged and humbled to have been part of that.

For us the story ended – but God's story for Ibiza will never end.

The 'Ibiza Sun' did an interview with Charlie Clayton, and as part of it they asked a few of the bar owners what they thought of 24-7 Ibiza. The following came from Sean Conway at The Huddle Bar in San Antonio:

'Hi Nick

Yes, I'm well aware of the work of 24/7.

I got to know Brian and Tracy when they first set up the Ibiza branch of the organisation ... one that I'd never heard of till that point. They we're out on the street handing out bits of fruit to workers and tourists. Naturally, I thought it was some kind of PR stunt for a club or bar, so was rather surprised to find out the truth.

As a tourist once put it to me ... "So, groups are just going round talking to people and then picking up drunks and taking them to their hotel or the hospital, and they're not selling anything?"

I've seen them, over the years, carry away hundreds of drunk, confused people and get them cared for. Many of them have been abandoned or become detached from a group of friends and left alone in the street. The majority of them have got themselves into their situation due to the over-indulgence in all that Ibiza has to offer. But, there's no questioning or moralising on the part of 24/7 ... they see someone in trouble and they're there to help.

I've seen them take abuse at times, get covered in vomit, questioned by the police and not receive a word of thanks from those they help. They've been accused of being a pirate taxi service and drug dealers, none of which have deterred them from their voluntary duty.

I suppose, in a way, they are PRs. Just not for a bar or a nightclub. Brian once told me that the best way they could spread the word of God, and how much he cares for us, was by showing a practical example of this to people.

The group continues, under new leadership, and they'll still be on the street tonight helping those that have over-indulged. The bar owners, police, ambulance staff and the casualties themselves, owe 24/7 a big debt of thanks.'